WAS CHRIST BORN IN BETHLEHEM?

A Study on the Credibility of St. Luke

WAS CHRIST BORN IN BETHLEHEM?

A Study on the Credibility of St. Luke

by
Sir William Ramsay, M.A., D.C.L.

LONDON: HODDER AND STROUGHTON
27 PATERNOSTER ROW
1898

ISBN: 978-1-6673-0606-3 paperback
ISBN: 978-1-6673-0607-0 hardcover

Dedicated
**TO THE MEMORY
OF MY UNCLE
ANDREW MITCHELL**

Preface

UNDERSTANDING that a certain criticism implied a sort of challenge to apply my theory of Luke's character as a historian to the Gospel, I took what is generally acknowledged to be the most doubtful passage, from the historian's view, in the New Testament, Luke 2:1-4. Many would not even call it doubtful. Strauss (in his *New Life of Jesus*) and Renan dismiss it in a short footnote as unworthy even of mention in the text.

This passage, interpreted according to the view which I have maintained – that Luke was a great historian, and that he appreciated the force of the Greek superlative (in spite of the contradiction of Professor Blass and others) – gave the result that Luke was acquainted with a system of Periodic Enrollments in Syria, and probably in the East generally. I looked for evidence of such a system; and it was offered by recent discoveries in Egypt. The confirmation afforded to Luke was explained in the *Expositor*, April and June, 1897.

Realizing better in subsequent thought the bearings of the Egyptian discovery, I have enlarged these two articles into an argument against the view that Luke sinks, in the accessories of his narrative, below the standard exacted from ordinary historians. At the risk of repeating views already stated in previous works, the second chapter attempts to put clearly the present state of the question as regards the two books of Luke, without expecting others to be familiar with my views already published.

The names of those scholars whose views I contend against are hardly ever mentioned. The scholars of the "destructive" school seem to prefer not to be mentioned, when one differs from them. I have learned much from them; I was once guided by them; I believe that the right understanding of the New Testament has been very greatly advanced by their laudable determination to probe and to understand everything, as is stated on p. 33; but I think their conclusions are to a great extent erroneous. It might, however, be considered disingenuous if I concealed that the weighty authority of Gardthausen, the historian of Augustus, is dead against me, p. 102.

My best thanks are due to Professor Paterson, who has discussed many points and cleared up my views in many ways; to Mr. B. P. Grenfell, who read the first proof of chapter 7, and enabled me to strengthen it; and, at last, to Mr. F. G. Kenyon; to Mr. A. C. Hunt; to Mr. Vernon Bartlett; and to Mr. A. Souter.

The language of the book has profited much by my wife's care in revision.

It would be impossible – and only wearisome to the reader if it were possible – to trace the origin of every thought expressed in the following pages. Where I was conscious, at the moment of writing, that I was using an idea suggested by another, I have said so; but as regards the New Testament, one learns in the course of years so much from so many sources that one knows not who is the teacher in each detail.

The relation between the almost identical solutions of the Quirinius difficulty, proposed nearly simultaneously by M. R. S. Bour and myself, is explained in chapter 11.

W. M. RAMSAY.

POSTSCRIPT. – I hear, Oct. 2, that Messrs. Grenfell and Hunt have found a household-enrollment paper a little older than AD. 50. The date is lost, but the same officials are mentioned in it as in a document of the 6th year of [Tiberius], where the names of Claudius and Caligula are impossible. Hence the paper belongs to the census of AD. 20, and proves conclusively my theory as to the origin of the Periodic Enrollments from Augustus. Much of the argument in chapter 7, printed when the Periodic Enrollments were traced with certainty only as far back as AD. 92, is now confirmed so completely, that part of it is hardly necessary.

Table of Contents

PART I. IMPORTANCE OF THE PROBLEM 9
    Chapter 1. LUKE'S HISTORY: WHAT IT PROFESSES TO BE 10
    Chapter 2. THE DESIGN AND UNITY OF LUKE'S HISTORY 20
    Chapter 3. LUKE'S ATTITUDE TOWARDS THE ROMAN WORLD 34
    Chapter 4. IMPORTANCE IN LUKE'S HISTORY OF THE STORY OF THE BIRTH OF CHRIST 47

PART II. SOLUTION OF THE PROBLEM 59
    Chapter 5. THE QUESTION AT ISSUE 60
    Chapter 6. LUKE'S ACCOUNT OF THE ENROLLMENT 72
    Chapter 7. ENROLLMENT BY HOUSEHOLDS IN EGYPT 80
    Chapter 8. THE SYRIAN ENROLLMENT IN 8 BC 90
    Chapter 9. KING HEROD'S ENROLLMENT 103
    Chapter 10. CHRONOLOGY OF THE LIFE OF CHRIST 115
    Chapter 11. QUIRINIUS THE GOVERNOR OF SYRIA 133

PART III. SOME ASSOCIATED QUESTIONS 145
    Chapter 12. SOME ASSOCIATED QUESTIONS 146

APPENDICES 156

PART I.
IMPORTANCE OF THE PROBLEM

Chapter 1.
LUKE'S HISTORY: WHAT IT PROFESSES TO BE

AMONG the writings which are collected in the New Testament, there is included a History of the life of Christ and of the first steps in the diffusion of his teaching through the Roman world, composed in two books. These two books have been separated from one another as if they were different works, and are ordinarily called "The Gospel according to Luke" and "The Acts of the Apostles". It is, however, certain from their language, and it is admitted by every scholar, that the two books were composed by a single author as parts of a single historical work on. a uniform plan. After a period of independent existence, this History in two books was incorporated in the Canon, and its unity was broken up: the first book was placed among the group of four Gospels, and the second was left apart.

Professor Blass has pointed out a trace of this original independent existence in the famous manuscript which was presented by the Reformer Beza to the University of Cambridge. In that manuscript the name of John is spelt in two different ways, the form Joanes being almost invariably used in Luke and Acts, and Joannes in the Gospels of Matthew, Mark and John.[1] That slight difference in orthography leads us back to the time of some old copyist, who used as his authority a manuscript of the History of Luke, in which the spelling Joanes was employed, and different manuscripts of the other Gospels containing the spelling Joannes. Probably the spelling Joanes was that employed by the original author; and it is adopted in Westcott and Hort›s edition throughout the New Testament, except in Acts 4:6 and Revelation 22:8.

This historical work in two books is attributed by tradition to Luke, the companion and pupil of Paul. We are not here concerned with that tradition. Since all scholars are agreed that the same author wrote both books, we shall use the traditional name to indicate him merely for the sake of brevity, as it is necessary to have some name by which to designate the author; but we shall found no argument upon the authorship. Like Professor Blass, I see no reason to doubt the tradition; but those who do not accept the tradition may treat the name Luke in these pages as a mere sign to indicate the author, whoever he may be.

The point with which we are here specially concerned is the trustworthiness of this author as a historian. Many facts are recorded by him alone, and it is a serious question whether or not they can be accepted on his sole authority.

This is a subject on which there prevails a good deal of misapprehension and even confusion of thought. There are many who seem to think that they show fairness of mind by admitting that Luke has erred in this point or in that, while they still cling to their belief in other things, which he and he alone, records, on the ground that in those cases there is no clear evidence against him. But it must be said that this way of reasoning is really mistaken and unjustifiable: it refuses to make the inference that necessarily follows from the first admission.

While human nature is fallible, and any man may make a slip in some unimportant detail, it is absolutely necessary to demand inexorably from a real historian accuracy in the essential and critical facts. We may pardon an occasional instance of bias or prejudice; for who is wholly free from it? But we cannot pardon any positive blunder in the really important points. If a historian is convicted of error in such a vital point, he ceases to be trustworthy on his own account; and every statement that he makes must gain credit from testimony external to him, or from general reasons and arguments, before we accept it. Especially must this be the case with the ancient historians, who as a rule hide their authorities and leave us in the dark as to the reasons and evidence that guided them to formulate their statements. There may be – there always are – many facts which the poorest chronicler records correctly; but we accept each of these, not because of the recorder's accurate and sound judgment in selecting his facts, but because of other reasons external to him. If there is in such a historian any statement that is neither supported nor contradicted by external evidence, it remains uncertain and is treated as possibly true, but it shares in the suspicion roused by the one serious blunder.

If we claim – and I have elsewhere in the most emphatic terms claimed – a high rank for Luke as regards trustworthiness, we must look fairly and squarely at the serious errors that are charged against him. If the case is proved against him in any of these, we must fairly admit the inevitable inference. If, on the other hand, we hold that the case is not proved, it is quite justifiable and reasonable, in a period of history so obscure as the first century, to plead, as many have done, that, while we cannot in the present dearth of information solve the difficulty completely, we are obliged, in accordance with our perception of the high quality of the author's work as a whole, to accept his statement in certain cases where he is entirely uncorroborated. These must for the present rank among the difficulties of Luke. There are difficulties in every important Greek author, and each difficulty is the scholar's opportunity.

But it must be the aim of those who believe in the high character of Luke's History, to discover new evidence which shall remove these difficulties and justify the controverted statements. The progress of discovery has recently placed in our hands the solution of one most serious difficulty and the justification of one much controverted statement; and the following pages are written with the intention of showing what is the bearing of this discovery on the general question as to the historical credibility of Luke.

The whole spirit and tone of modern commentaries on Luke's writings depend on the view which the commentators take on this question. In some cases the commentator holds that no historical statement made by Luke is to be believed, unless it can be proved from authorities independent of him. The commentary on Luke then degenerates into a guerrilla warfare against him; the march of the narrative is interrupted at every step by a series of attacks in detail. Hardly any attempt is made to estimate as a whole, or to determine what is the most favourable interpretation that can be placed on any sentence in the work. There is a manifest predilection in favor of the interpretation which is discordant with external facts or with other statements in Luke. If it is possible to

PART I. Importance of the Problem

read into a sentence a meaning which contradicts another passage in the same author, that is at once assumed to be the one intended by him; and his incapacity and untrustworthiness are illustrated in the commentary.

But no work of literature could stand being treated after this fashion. Imagine the greatest of pagan authors commented on in such a way; any slip of expression exaggerated or distorted; sentences strained into contradiction with other passages of the same or other authors; the commentary directed to magnify every fault, real or imaginary, but remaining silent about every excellence. There have occasionally been such commentaries written about great classical authors; and they have always been condemned by the general consent of scholars. Even where the bias of the commentator was due to a not altogether unhealthy revolt against general over-estimate of the author under discussion, the world of scholarship has always recognized that the criticism which looks only for faults is useless, misleading, unprogressive, and that. it defeats itself, when it tries to cure an evil by a much greater evil. Scholarship and learning sacrifice their vitality, and lose all that justifies their existence, when they cease to be fair and condescend to a policy of "malignity".

In this discussion it is obviously necessary to conduct the investigation as one of pure history, to apply to it the same canons of criticism and interpretation that are employed in the study of the other ancient historians, and to regard as our subject, not "the Gospel according to Luke," but the History composed by Luke. The former name is apt to suggest prepossession and prejudice: the latter is purely critical and dispassionate.

In estimating the character and qualities of an author we must look first of all to his opportunities. Had he good means of reaching the truth, or was his attempt to attain thorough knowledge of the facts made in the face of great difficulties? An historian ought to give us a statement of his own claims to be received as trustworthy, or an estimate of the character of the evidence which he had at his disposal.

Luke has not failed to put clearly before his readers what character he claims for his history. He has given us, in the prefatory paragraph of his Gospel, a clear statement of the intention with which he wrote his history, and of the qualifications which give him the right to be accepted as an authority. He was not an eye-witness of the remarkable events which he is proceeding to record, but was one of the second generation to whom the information had been communicated by those "who were from the beginning eye-witnesses and ministers of the word". The simplest interpretation of his words is that he claims to have received much of his information from the mouths of eye-witnesses; and, on careful study of the preface as a whole, it seems impossible to avoid the conclusion that he deliberately makes this claim. Any other interpretation, though it might be placed on one clause by itself, is negatived by the drift of the paragraph as a whole.

Thus Luke claims to have had access to authorities of the first rank, persons who had seen and heard and acted in the events which he records. He makes no distinction as to parts of his narrative. He claims the very highest authority for it as a whole.

In the second place, Luke claims to have studied and comprehended every event in its origin and development, (παρηκολουθηκότι ἄνωθεν πᾶσιν ἀκριβῶς) *i.e.*, to have investigated the preliminary circumstances, the genesis and growth of what he writes about. Exactness and definiteness of detail in his narrative – these are implied in the word ἄνωθεν: investigation and personal study implied in the word παρηκολουθηκότι: tracing of events from their causes and origin – implied in ἄνωθεν: such are the qualities which Luke declares to be his justification for writing a narrative, when many other narratives already were in existence; and he says emphatically that this applies to all that he narrates.

The expression used clearly implies that Luke began to write his narrative, because he was already in possession of the knowledge gained by study and investigation; as he begins, he is in the position of one who already has acquired the information needed for his purpose. This is implied in the perfect παρηκολουθηκότι. The rendering in the Authorized and the Revised Version does not bring this out quite clearly: from the English words – "it seemed good to me also, having traced the course of all things accurately from the first,[2] to write unto thee in order» –

one might infer that the study and tracing of the course of events was resolved upon with the view of writing the history. But in the Greek that meaning would require the aorist participle. With the perfect participle the meaning must be «as I already possess the knowledge, it seemed good to me, like the others, to write a formal narrative for your use.»

On this point, I am glad to find myself in agreement with Professor Sanday, who refuses to assume that Luke "began with the intention of writing a history, and accumulated materials deliberately in view of this intention all through his career". We cannot assume that, for the author, by implication, denies it. But we may safely assume that he had both the intelligent curiosity of an educated[3] Greek, and the eager desire for knowledge about the facts of the Saviour›s life, natural in a believer who rested his faith and his hopes on the life and death of Christ.

Possibly some one may say that it is assuming too much when I speak of the author as an "educated" Greek. But any one who knows Greek can gather that from the preface alone. No one who had not real education and feeling for style could have written that sentence, so well balanced, expressed in such delicately chosen terms, so concise, and so full of meaning.

In the third place, Luke declares his intention to give a comprehensive narrative of the events in order from first to last (καθεξῆς σοι γράψαι). This does not necessarily imply a chronological order but a rational order, making things comprehensible, omitting nothing that is essential for full and proper understanding. In a narrative so arranged it stands to reason that, in general, the order will be chronological, though of course the order of logical exposition sometimes overrides simple chronological sequence (see chapter 10). Further, it is involved in the idea of a well-arranged History that the scale on which each event is narrated should be according to its importance in the general plan.

Finally the account which Luke gives is, as he emphatically declares, trustworthy and certain (ἵνα ἐπιγνῷς τὴν ἀσφάλειαν). His expression indubitably implies that he was not entirely satisfied with the existing narratives. He does not, it is true, say that explicitly; he utters no word of criticism on his predecessors, and he declares that they got their information from eye-witnesses. But his expression distinctly implies that he considered that some advance was still to be made, either as regards completeness, or as regards orderly exposition of the facts, or as regards accuracy. In all probability the fault in the existing narratives which Luke had especially in mind was their incompleteness. They embodied the tradition of eye-witnesses and ministers of the Word "from the beginning" (ἀπ' ἀρχῆς), which seems to imply "the beginning of the preaching of the Word". We have to think of narratives in the form of the Gospel of Mark, with the opening: "the beginning of the Gospel of Jesus Christ" – narratives that commence with some such stage as the baptism. In contrast to these narratives Luke claims to trace the whole series of events from their origin, *i.e.*, from the higher or preliminary stage out of which they were derived ἄνωθεν).

It seems beyond doubt that, in speaking of the origin, Luke has in view the narrative which he proceeds to give of the birth and early days of the Savior. Therein lay the most serious addition that he made to the narratives of his predecessors; and for that addition in particular he claims the same high character as for the narrative as a whole: he has it from firstclass authorities – exact, complete and trustworthy (see chapter 4).

In view of the emphatic claim which Luke makes, that his whole narrative rests on the highest authority and is accurate and certain, it is obvious that we cannot agree with the attitude of those scholars, who, while accepting this whole History as the work of the real Luke, the follower and disciple and physician and intimate friend of Paul, are wont to write about the inadequacy of his authorities, the incompleteness of his information, the puzzling variation in the scale and character of his narrative according as he had good or inferior authorities to trust to. The writer of the preface would not admit that view: he claims to state throughout what is perfectly trustworthy.

It may be allowed, consistently with his own claim, that his information was not everywhere equally good and complete. Thus, for example, he would naturally have heard much more about the facts of the Savior's life, than about the events of the few years that followed upon his death: attention would be concentrated on the former, and the latter would be much less thought about or inquired into. But this view cannot be carried far without coming into contradiction with the profession of the preface. And, above all, those who admit that the Luke of the Epistles, the friend and companion of Paul, was the author of this History must not attempt to explain the account given by Luke of important events in Paul's life, such as the Apostolic Council (Acts 15, by the supposition that the author was not acquainted with Paul's account of the facts and character of that most critical event. He who had been Paul's companion during the stormy years following that Council, when its decision was the subject of keen debate and rival interpretations, must have known what were Paul's views on the subject.

It is important to note that Luke in this preface distinguishes between the written accounts and the tradition of the eye-witnesses (καθὼς παρέδοσαν οἱ αὐτόπται). So far as the actual word tradition, or Paradosis, goes, it might, and in many cases does, refer to written narrative; but in the present case the logic of the passage clearly implies a pointed distinction between tradition and written narrative. There existed when Luke wrote, on the one hand, oral tradition from eye-witnesses, and, on the other hand, many narratives written by those who learned from the eye-witnesses and put the tradition in literary form; but there were as yet no written narratives composed by eye-witnesses. This inference is drawn by Professor Blass, and is distinctly implied in Luke's preface. Luke may have known Mark's Gospel, and probably used it; but he did not know the other two Gospels.

There can only be one conclusion, when the terms of Luke's preface are duly weighed. Either an author who begins with a declaration such as that had mixed freely with many of the eye-witnesses and actors in the events which he proceeds to record, or he is a thorough impostor, who consciously and deliberately aims at producing belief in his exceptional qualifications in order to gain credit for his History. The motive for such an imposture could hardly be mere empty desire to be considered a true narrator. The man of that age, who was deliberately outraging truth, felt no such overpowering passion for the distinction of having attained abstract truth in history. He must have sought to put on the semblance of truth and authority in order to gain some end by conciliating belief in his narrative; he must have desired to gain credit in order that his party or his opinions might triumph. They who declare that the author belonged to a later age are bound to prove that there was some such intention in his mind.

Hitherto every attempt to show that the historian had such an aim in view has ended in complete failure. With regard to Book I., the Gospel, the attempt is ludicrous; the narrative is so transparently simple and natural that hardly any amount of prepossession could read into it such aims. With Book II., the Acts, we are not here concerned. Elsewhere I have tried to show what a single eye the author has in that book to the simple statement of facts as they actually happened; it seems to me to be almost as transparently simple and natural as the Gospel.

No rational theory, such as would for a moment be admitted in regard to an ordinary classical author, has ever been advanced to account for the supposition of deliberate imposture in the claims to credit advanced by Luke. If the author was an impostor, his work remains one of the most incomprehensible and unintelligible facts in literary history. One can imagine, for example, that Peter was written by a person who was so filled with the conviction that he was giving the views of his master, Peter the Apostle, as to express the letter in Peter's name; the case might seem to him (from a mistaken point of view) to be not wholly unlike the expression of the old prophets, "thus saith the Lord". That is a conceivable and rational hypothesis, though whether it be true or false we cannot say, and need not now inquire. No such rational hypothesis has yet been advanced to account for Luke's far more elaborate, and therefore more deliberate, imposture.

But this abstract and rather intangible argument must yield to the demonstration of hard facts. So much we freely grant. Now it is asserted that the historian whom we are studying has been guilty of such serious and gross blunders, when he touches on matters of general history, that his information cannot have been so good as he pretends, and therefore he must be claiming too much when he arrogates such an authoritative character for his History. We shall feel bound to accept that argument; and, if the blunders are demonstrated, we must accept the necessary inferences and abandon our championship of his accuracy and trustworthiness. But let us first examine the demonstration.

We cannot investigate in this volume every "blunder" that is charged against Luke; but we shall treat one rather fully. If I may judge both from personal feeling, from conversation, and from many books, the "blunder" which most contributes to rouse prejudice against him as an historian, occurs at the very beginning, in that same episode on which he evidently lays such stress in his preface – the story of the Birth of Christ. In this story the enrollment or census of Palestine in the time of Quirinius is a critical point; and the doubt whether any such census as Luke describes was made, is the cause of important and far-reaching results. It is declared to be a blunder, or rather a complication of blunders; and if that be so, the entire story must be relegated to the realm of mythology, and the writer who mistakes fable for fact, and tries to prop up his mistake by an error of the grossest kind, can retain no credit as an historical authority.

In conclusion, we shall briefly refer to one or two other typical so-called "errors" in Luke.

---

[1] Exceptions – one in Luke, two each in Matthew, Mark and Acts, seven in John.
[2] Better «from their origin».
[3] *Expositor*, Feb., 1896, p. 90.

Chapter 2.
THE DESIGN AND UNITY OF LUKE'S HISTORY

AS has been stated, a historian may make a slip in some detail without losing claim to be trustworthy: no man and no historian is perfect. But he must not found his reasoning upon the error. Facts that are fundamental in his argument must be free from slip or fault. There must be no mistake on a critical point.

If we consider Luke's design, we shall see that the "error" which forms our subject affects the very life-blood of the work and the atmosphere in which the story moves. But every great work of literature like Luke's History must be reinterpreted by each new age for itself; and it is more useful to describe what views are now held as to the plan and design of that History, than to sketch the design.

The consummate literary skill shown in Luke's work must impress every reader, who allows free play to his sense of literary effect. We feel that in this work we have to deal with an author who handles his materials freely and with perfect mastery. The unity of style and treatment in the narrative, its dramatic character, varying according to the country and the action and the character of every speaker, so Greek in Athens, so "provincial" in the Roman colonies Lystra and Philippi, so Hebraic in Galilee or by the Jordan, and so Lukan everywhere – this character and individuality, shown in numberless ways, make it clear that the author was no clipper-up of fragments from other writers, no mere scissors-and-paste editor of scraps, no mere second-hand composer, dependent on the accidental character of his "sources," according to the elaborate and somewhat pedantic theories that have been fashionable recently in Germany, but are already becoming discredited there. Only a person who has blinded himself to literary feeling by the strength of a fixed prejudice, could fail to perceive the literary quality of this History, and to infer from it the real unity of the work.

PART I. Importance of the Problem

When a commentator on the text of Luke, observing that Luke "can be as Hebraistic as the Septuagint and as free from Hebraisms as Plutarch," and that "he is Hebraistic in describing Hebrew society," and Greek in describing Greek society, refrains from expressing any opinion as to whether this result is attained "intentionally or not," that is a very proper reserve for a commentator to maintain. He is not called upon to determine in the preface to a commentary whether this varying character has been given intentionally to the work by its author, or has remained attached to it by chance, according as the character of the different documents on which Luke depended continued to exist in his completed work. But the literary judgment will not hesitate. Luke is so completely master of his materials, and handles the Greek language with such ease and power, that he must have intended to give his work the literary qualities which are observable in it. A rational criticism must always assume that an author intended to attain that delicately graduated effect which in fact he has attained.

But the interval which separated the historian from the events which he records is an important element in estimating his design. Great literary power may tell against his trustworthiness, by helping him to hide the poverty of his materials; and that view has been maintained as regards Luke by writers of the type of Baur, Zeller and Renan. They argued that Luke was an able and beautiful but not very well-informed author, who lived long after the events which he records, at a time when all actors in those events had died, and when accurate knowledge of facts was difficult to acquire. In addition to the skillful arguments by which they showed up a series of internal discrepancies and improbabilities, the apparent discordance between the narrative (especially in the second book) and the general scheme and character of Roman Imperial administration in the Eastern provinces, seemed to many to weigh heavily against the idea that the book embodied a really trustworthy account of events.

In the picture of Christian history during the first century, according to the accepted interpretation of Luke's History, there was no apparent relation between the development of Christian influence and the existing facts of the Roman empire. The modern writers who professed to found their views upon Luke, after a few picturesque paragraphs about Roman proconsuls and armies and the march of the Roman eagles, plunged into Christian history, and the reader saw nothing more of Rome except when a Gallio or a Sergius Paullus obtruded himself on the scene with something of the air of a bad actor equipped in ill-fitting Roman dress. The life of the empire was wanting: that consisted, not in eagles and proconsuls, but in order and organization, and in the development and Romanisation of society.

Those who studied Roman history first of all, and Christian history only in a secondary degree, were inevitably driven to the conclusion that a work, upon which was founded such a lifeless and spiritless picture of part of the Roman world in the first century, could not be a product of that century, but must have originated at a later date, when the life of the time described was no longer understood.

But a most important part of Luke's Second Book is concerned with Asia Minor and Greece; and any one who has gone through the long, slow process by which in recent years the lost history of Asia Minor has been in some degree recreated by the work of a number of scholars, and their studies Luke without prepossession, must observe, that his references to those lands have a marked and peculiar individuality – a certain matter-of-fact tone – which is utterly unlike the vague style of a later author, narrating the events of a past age with the purpose of showing their bearing on the questions of his own day. One feels that, in all that concerns Asia Minor, Luke is treating real facts with thorough knowledge.

As knowledge of Asia Minor grew, one perceived that Luke's statements explained some most obscure problems by setting in a new light the evidence that had long seemed unintelligible. Luke takes us right into the midst of the political development of central Asia Minor, when Roman organizing skill was treating one by one the successive problems of government amid a semi-Oriental population, regarding some districts as still too rude to be Romanised, and placing them under the educative care of dependent kings, treating others as already worthy of

PART I. Importance of the Problem

the honor of being incorporated in the Roman empire as fractions of a great province, and fostering among them a spirit of pride in the Imperial connection and contempt for the extra-provincial barbarians.

It is a difficult thing to revivify and rearrange the details of that magnificent political work; and in some respects I erred in my first attempt[4] to recreate the picture of the Imperial scheme for Romanising the inner lands by gradually building them up into a great Roman province called Galatia. But the errors (though vexatious to myself as I gradually came to see more clearly) were not so important as to disturb materially the truth of the picture in its general effect. It had been given me, through intense longing after truth, to catch the main outlines correctly, and to understand that Luke's brief references to the state of central Asia Minor plunged the reader into the heart of the conflict between Graeco-Roman forms of life and the amorphous barbarism of a Phrygian and Lycaonian population. In that state of the land, to be Phrygian or Lycaonian was to be unenlightened and non-Roman, to be Roman was to be a loyal member of the province Galatia. Such a state of things could not have been conceived or understood by a writer of the second century, when Rome had long been supreme over the whole of Asia Minor, and when the opposition between the contending ideas, Roman or Galatic on the one hand, native (*i.e.*, Phrygian, Pisidian, etc.) and non-Roman on the other, had ceased to be a real force in the country.

But if this view which opened gradually before us was correct, then we had to abandon the current, generally accepted opinion, which. admitted no Roman conceptions in the terms relating to geography and political classification in Acts, which saw, for example, in the "Galatic Territory," not a Roman province, but the country where Attalus, King of Pergamos, had confined the Galatae or Galli about 230 BC. We must regard Paul as a Roman, using Roman terms and forms, just as he accepted the Roman classification and system of administration.

As it happened, this implied and necessitated a radical revolution in the interpretation of the book of Acts and of early Christian history as a whole. It meant that the connection and the conflict between Christianity and the Roman State did not begin in the second century, as was the almost unanimous opinion of the greatest authorities during the halfcentury preceding 1890 (when Neumann's book carried back the beginning to the reign of Domitian, AD. 81-96). It meant that the conscious and recognized relations between the New Religion and the Roman Administration began when Barnabas and Saul stood before the Roman proconsul of Cyprus, when the latter, hitherto junior and subordinate to Barnabas, took the lead, and the supposed Hebrew wise man named Saul stood forth as the Greek Paul and impressed the Roman governor by declaring the principles of the new Catholic, world-wide religion. It meant that the first important step in the spreading of this Catholic religion was made, when Paul and Barnabas crossed Taurus from the secluded and unimportant Province Pamphylia, into the important Province Galatia – the province which embodied all that was Roman in Central Asia Minor, the province in which the Roman element was involved in the sharpest antagonism to the rude ignorance of an Oriental, priest-guided, ritual-loving native population – and planted their feet on the great highway of intercourse between the East and the West.

Further, it now began to grow clear that some of the discrepancies which had been the mainstay of Baur's and Zeller's argument, were due to the stereotyped misunderstanding of the Roman side of early Christian history, Both the general character and many details of that history were distorted, when contemplated through the medium of the dominant theory.

The life of the early Church lay in constant intercommunication between all its parts; its health and growth were dependent on the free circulation of the life-blood of common thought and feeling. Hence it was first firmly seated on the great lines of communication across the empire, leading from its origin in Jerusalem to its imperial center in Rome. It had already struck root in Rome within little more than twenty years after the crucifixion, and it had become really strong in the great city about thirty years after the apostles began to look round and out from Jerusalem. This marvelous development was possible only because the seed of the new thought floated free on the main currents of communication, which were ever sweeping back and forward between the heart of the empire and its outlying members. Paul, who mainly directed the great movement, threw himself boldly and confidently into the life of the time; he took the empire as it was, accepted its political conformation and arrangement, and sought only to touch the spiritual and moral life of the people, while he always advised them to obey the existing Government and conform to the existing laws of the State and of society, so far as they did not lead into direct conflict with Christian principles.

But the formerly accepted interpretation of the Second Book of Luke's History carried Christianity away into eddies and backwaters of the ocean of Roman Imperial development, and placed there the scene of the first great conflict between Judaistic provincialism and the world-wide Pauline conception of Christianity. It was blind to the true character of Paul's work, which sought to spiritualize the life and educative development of the empire by affecting the main currents of its circulation and intercommunication; and it tried to distinguish the lines along which the new thought spread from the lines along which the life of the world was throbbing.

The dominance of that interpretation produced a position, the analogue of which still exists in respect of some other questions. That theory led straight into a series of difficulties, for which no rationally satisfying solution could be found; and the scholars who treated Luke's History were divided broadly into two classes. Some saw so clearly the unity, the power and the personal quality in the work, that they refused to be led astray by the serious difficulties in which they were involved on certain points. Others realized so strongly the difficulties, that they formed their judgment from them alone and ignored the quality of the History as a whole.

The progress of discovery is indubitably tending to show that the scholars of the former class were, on the whole, in the right; but this should not blind us to the immense service rendered by those of the other class, who kept the difficulties clear before the world's consciousness.

Moreover, it must be admitted that the scholars who judged by literary feeling and the general quality of Luke's History, were not always wise in their treatment of the difficulties. Instead of frankly acknowledging that the difficulties were inexplicable in our present state of knowledge, they sometimes attempted by ingenious special pleading to minimize them, and then claimed that the difficulties were solved. Their vigorous perception of the central and most important fact, *viz.*, the first-hand directness of Luke's style, made them so thoroughly convinced that the difficulties must be explicable, that they were almost blinded to the strength of the arguments against them, and sometimes thought they had explained difficulties, when they had merely shut their eyes to them.

The result was that those who, like myself, had been accustomed only to classical Greek, and were too young to appreciate fully the literary quality of a writer in such an unfamiliar form of Greek, and who were determined to understand clearly and precisely every step in reasoning, were repelled by what seemed to us to be pure prejudice and unwillingness to admit reason, and were driven violently over to the opposite side; and it was a long and slow process to work back again to the side against which we had acquired such a strong prepossession.

In such a state of mind it was natural to rest for a time in a theory of double authorship, that Luke's History was partly excellent and partly second-rate (as I was almost inclined to do while writing *The Church in the Roman Empire*).¹ One could feel that Luke's Second Book was characterized by such singular accuracy in all details bearing on the society and the political organization of the Eastern provinces, that the author's expression in many places could not have been framed without first-hand knowledge, and that his point of view was distinctly of the first century, or rather the pre-Domitianic type, as distinguished from that which was produced by the persecution of Domitian.

But, on the other hand, parts of the History seemed to involve insoluble difficulties and discrepancies.

Hence, while no distinct theory was stated in my treatise, yet the language used in it sometimes pointed towards a theory of dual authorship.

But such ideas were utterly inconsistent with the unity of plan, the vigorous controlling intellect which revealed itself throughout Luke's work; and the impossibility to stand still in such a halfway position, clinging to rival and inconsistent views, became rapidly manifest. It was not possible to introduce maturer views into the book already published, even in a new edition; for the sole merit that it possessed lay in its being perfectly unprejudiced and unfettered by any theory as to the composition of Luke's History. After forming a definite opinion about that History as a whole, it was no longer possible to write as if one had no opinion. Therefore, the book had to remain as it was, with its defect of being not self-consistent in respect of Luke, since the want of systematic unity was the guarantee of its being the unprejudiced effort of a mind groping for truth.

It became more and more clear that it is impossible to divide Luke's History into parts, attributing to one portion the highest authority as the first-hand narrative of a competent and original authority, while regarding the rest as of quite inferior mold. If the author of one part is the real Luke, or any other person standing in similar close relations with the circle surrounding the apostles (particularly Paul), then that same person must be the author of the whole, and must have brought to bear on his whole work the same qualities which made one part so excellent. It may be that he found it more difficult to feel perfectly at home in the Palestinian part of his narrative than where the scene lies in the Aegean lands. It may be that in the parts intervening between the Resurrection or the Ascension (with which many, probably all, of his written authorities ended) and the beginning of Paul's personal recollections, he found it harder to obtain perfectly satisfactory knowledge. But we cannot lay much stress on these causes of diversity in character. The History must stand as a whole, and be judged as a whole. If one part shows striking historical excellence, so must all; if any part shows a conspicuous historical blunder, we must be very suspicious of a theory which attributes surpassing qualities to another part.

In regard to the Second Book of Luke, my arguments are set forth elsewhere,[5] and, while I feel conscious how imperfectly they have been stated, and how much better the work ought to have been done, I have nothing of consequence either to retract or to modify, though much might be added. After three years more of study, Luke appears more clearly than ever to me as one of the great historians.

Such a view is unfashionable; and there is in some quarters a disposition to regard it even as a crime and a personal affront to the distinguished scholars who have thought differently. It is true that I have advocated a view diametrically opposed to their judgment, and that, if I be right, they have erred in a critical question of the utmost importance and interest. But I have not sought to give the discussion this personal application. It is not a crime to differ from another scholar as to the date and quality of any of the disputed classical works; and my desire has been to proceed in regard to Luke on the same lines as in the questions of extra-Biblical scholarship. One of the scholars whom I reverence most deeply in all Europe differs very strongly from my judgment as to the authority of the *Peutinger Table*, but the difference makes no change in my profound respect and admiration for him, and none in the great kindness which he has always shown to a beginner like me. Similarly there is no reason why Luke's authority as a historian should not be treated as a justifiable subject for discussion. I entertain, and have always professed, great admiration for many scholars whose opinions I dispute on some points of Christian history, and from their learning I have gained much.

It is a more serious evil that a disposition is sometimes shown to terrorize the investigator by the array of learned opinion on the opposite side, and to treat it as the necessary mark of a reasonable scholar in this subject, that he should be always searching for and finding proofs of the late date, and inaccuracy, and composite character of Luke's History. It is comforting to certain minds to have some one whose opinions they can accept implicitly; and it would almost appear that a few of our English scholars attribute to the German commentators on the Bible that inerrancy which our parents or grandparents attributed to the text. They set up an idol, and condemn as an impious iconoclast him that sees the idol's feet of clay, even while he reverences the image.

But in matters of scholarship it is not safe to follow implicitly any scholar, however great he may be; and we appeal to fact and reason against the dogmatism which seeks to close the case, refuses to admit further argument, and brands as an "apologist" any defender of Luke's character as a historian.

Not long ago it was reckoned by many as essential to a respectable scholar that he should pooh-pooh Luke as a second-century writer. Now we are permitted, on the highest German authority, to date him in the first century. We are permitted also to speak of certain parts and scenes in the Second Book of his History as showing marvelous accuracy and great power of conceiving and setting before the reader a life-like picture of what actually occurred. But we are not permitted to infer that he is a trustworthy historian, and that the presumption is in favor of his accuracy, even in cases, where no clear external evidence corroborates his statements.

We might ask whether it is a probable or possible view that the author can be so unequal to himself, that in one place he can show very high qualities as an accurate historian, and that in another place, when dealing with events equally within the range of his opportunities for acquiring knowledge, he can prove himself incompetent to distinguish between good and bad, true and false. He that shows the historic faculty in part of his work has it as a permanent possession.

The power of vivid conception and accurate description in concise, wellchosen, pregnant language, which Luke admittedly shows in some passages, proves that he could estimate correctly the comparative importance of details, select the essential points, and skillfully group them. An author fixes a standard for himself at his best, and is most unlikely to sink below it. The true critic will recognize this, and will not rest satisfied till he has traced the same qualities throughout the work. That method of studying Luke has not yet been consistently employed in the light of modern historical, geographical and antiquarian knowledge. The attempt to carry it out consistently will be stigmatized by those who dislike its results as pedantic insistence on minute points of language and mere "Mikrologie"; but it must be made in the face of such prohibition.

On this subject there are only two alternatives. It grows more and more clear that compromise – such as is common among those by whom it is esteemed fair-minded to accept as much as possible from the results of the destructive school – is impossible. The mind that is really logical and self-consistent cannot admit part of the so-called "critical" view – what ought to be called the uncritical view – and yet on the whole cling to the belief in real Lukan authorship. Luke's History is of such a strongly marked character what are called the "gaps" or omissions in it are so distinct, or, in other words, the proportion of the parts in it is so peculiars – the insistence upon some facts and the summary dismissal of others with a bare word forms so prominent a feature of the work – that either the author had a distinct idea of plan and purpose and comparative importance, according to which his whole narrative was ordered and guided, or he was not the real Luke.

Occasionally it is possible, with some plausible and deceptive show of reason, to maintain that the length at which some incident is narrated is due merely to the author's possessing exceptionally good sources of information about it. Take for example, the long description of the voyage From Philippi to Caesarea. That description is given in the words of one who was present on the ships. It therefore rests on authority of the highest character; and it might plausibly be maintained that the exceptionally excellent nature of the information led the author to devote an exceptional amount of space to it.

But if a believer in the Lukan authorship of the History attempts in a consistent way to carry out that theory, he is led into hopeless contradiction. Situations at which the real Luke must have been present are dismissed in the curtest way or omitted altogether, while others in which he was not present are described at great length. If the author so carefully chronicles the progress past Chios, and Samos, and Cos, and Rhodes, and Myra, and Cyprus, for the sole reason that he was present and knew what happened, why should he, after describing so carefully and minutely the progress of the Gospel in Corinth and Ephesus, or its comparative failure in Athens, which he had not seen, sum up in a word the two years in Rome, where he was present – years which must have been so full of important events and impressive preaching? Why should he omit the two years' residence in Caesarea, except as regards two isolated scenes, and describe so much more fully the previous twelve days' residence there? Why should events in which Paul and Luke were both keenly interested, and as to which they must have known each other's views – why should such events be narrated at great length by Luke, and in a way which shows, on the accepted interpretation, utter ignorance of Paul's views?

No answer has ever been given to these questions. In truth, he who admits that theory must., if he is logical, go on, like Professor Harnack and Professor McGiffert, to deny that the real Luke was the author.

But it is at once the special strength and the peculiar weakness of English scholarship that, even when it makes a mistake, it shrinks with a healthy and saving instinct from carrying out the mistake to extremes; it is not consistent with itself where to be consistent means to go further astray. With its practical sense it gains the chief result – truth in the main. It returns to the right path when its course is becoming clearly divergent; and often it returns before it has erred so far from the true path as to become completely conscious of its wandering. Hence, it disapprovingly regards him that remonstrates with it for its want of consistency, on the ground that "he hunts down the statements of his opponents into what seem to him to be their consequences". In this country we are, perhaps, too apt to think that a scholar is responsible only for what he has explicitly stated, and not for the logical consequences of his views.

On the other hand, it is at once the strength and the weakness of German scholarship that it is thoroughly and remorselessly logical, that it carries out its views with steadfast and unwavering consistency, that it works out every theory to its consequences, that it is always conscious where it has gone, and is never untrue to itself, even though it thereby sacrifices the real object of its pursuit. When it goes wrong it demonstrates its own error with absolute conclusiveness, for it never works round out of the straight line back towards the true path.

A good example of the attempt at compromise and of the illogicality of such an attempt, is found in the main subject of our investigation – Luke's story of the birth of Christ and the first enrollment of Palestine.

The attack directed against the credibility of that episode has been strong, confident, almost triumphant in its tone.[6] The defense has been rather timid and hesitating; the introduction of Quirinius›s name has been abandoned almost universally as a demonstrated blunder; and even the reality of the «First Enrollment» has been championed by Luke›s advocates in a very reluctant and half-hearted way.

But to make even one of these concessions is practically and logically to abandon the case, so far as Luke's character as a historian is concerned. He who says that "Luke is in error in the name of Quirinius," admits that, even when Luke had learned a fact from some authority, he could not keep himself free from a huge blunder in stating it.

Beyond all doubt, the suspicion entertained about Luke's History is due to the belief that, when he touches on general history, his references are usually demonstrably false, as contrary to historical record, and are rarely or never conclusively supported by other historians. He is the only Evangelist who has attempted to place his narrative in its proper relation to contemporary history; and when he tries to do so, almost every one, even most of his defenders, admit that he cannot do it without making errors.

It is generally admitted that (as Canon Gore puts it) "the chronological data in Luke 2 and 3 were supplied by himself and not by his sources". Luke gives us the result of his own investigations into the historical surroundings of the life of Christ. But if his investigations were of such a character that he confused the census of 8 BC. with that of 6-7 AD., and imagined that Christ was born "in the days of Herod the King," during a census held about ten or eleven years after the death of Herod – when Herod was king, and yet when a Roman viceroy was organizing the new province of Palestine – of what value were his investigations, or his ideas about past history, or his evidence?[7] What should we think of the historical qualities of a modern author who began an account of the life of Hereward the Wake by confusing between Edward the Confessor and William the Conqueror? The one case would be no worse than the other. The first attempt that the author makes to connect his subject with contemporary history shows hopeless ignorance of that history.

It is no wonder in these circumstances that Luke's History has fallen under suspicion so strong that the case in its favor has been generally considered weaker than that in favor of any other important book in the New Testament. When I ventured, in defiance of the general verdict, to argue that Luke is a real historian – and "the first and the essential quality of the great historian is truth" – even so conservative and so friendly a scholar as Professor Sanday found that my "treatment of Luke as a historian seems too optimistic".

But it is an essentially inconsistent position to fancy that we can accept three-fourths or nine-tenths of what Luke says as true, and reject the rest. Destroy a historian's credit in one critical point, and there remains naught.

The confounding of one census with another in this case would be one of the serious things, which condemn the would-be historian as hopelessly incapable of accuracy or sound historical judgment. His statements cease to have any value in themselves; we can in each case only seek for a source, and estimate the probability of the statement by the authority of the source, after subtracting the likelihood of some other blunder having been made by Luke in using his source.

To judge how seriously this blunder affects the author's character, how inevitable are the inferences which the logical mind must deduce from the blunder, we must glance at two preliminary points which will form the subject of chapters 3. and 4.

---

[4] *The Church in the Roman Empire*, Pt. 1.
[5] Both in the pages of the *Expositor* in many separate articles, and in *St. Paul the Traveler and the Roman Citizen*.
[6] See chapter 5.
[7] There are other impossibilities upon impossibilities which have often been stated, and are repeated in chapter 5.

Chapter 3.
LUKE'S ATTITUDE TOWARDS THE ROMAN WORLD

The reign of Augustus, as is well known, is enveloped in the deepest obscurity. While we are unusually well informed about the immediately preceding period of Roman history, and for part of the reign of his successor, Tiberius, we possess the elaborate and accurate, though in some respects strongly prejudiced account of Tacitus, the facts of Augustus's reign have to be pieced together from scanty, incomplete and disjointed authorities.

Moreover, obscure events in a remote corner of the Roman world can never even in the best attested periods be expected to come within the purview of Roman history. Such events are preserved to us only by some accidental reference or some local authority; and it is unreasonable to cast doubt on the local authority, either because he relates what is not related by the Roman historians, or because he regards things from a different point of view, and sees them in different perspective, and applies to them a very different scale of importance.

The real value of these accidentally preserved local authorities is that they do *not* give the Roman point of view, but enable us to contemplate part of the Roman world, as it was seen by non-Roman eyes. What would we not give for a review of Caesar›s Gallic campaigns by a leading Gaulish Druid or chief, or for a criticism of Agricola by the chief bard of Boadicea or of Galgacus? Tacitus, indeed, has expressed the views of Galgacus, but we feel that it is Tacitus, not the British chief, that speaks.

We should, undoubtedly, find in the words of the Gaul or the Briton a very different view from the official justification and. *Apologia* for his career published by Caesar, or the panegyric composed by Tacitus. We should certainly have considerable difficulty in reconciling the opposing authorities, and in striking a balance between the discrepant judgments and statements as to facts. But it would be sheer unreason to set aside as mere invention every assertion of the Gallic or British authority, which could not be established on Roman authority. Reasonable and sound criticism will apply the same standard to Luke›s history. It will not demand that he, a Greek of the wider Greek world, as distinguished from the narrower country of Greece proper, should look at everything through Roman spectacles, and express everything precisely as a Roman would do. It will rate his value all the higher, because he has not done that – because he shows us how Roman things were looked at by one who was not a Roman. It will be prepared to find differences of expression and description, even when the Greek and the Roman are looking at the same historical fact. To estimate Luke fairly, it will ask what was his attitude towards the Roman world. In answer to this question, one might say much; but even a brief chapter may be of some use.

On the whole, Luke's view has in essentials a strong Paulinistic character. He was disposed towards the Imperial government and political institutions very much as Paul was, and as the wider Greek world in general was. He accepted unreservedly the existing facts of society and organization. But there was a difference between them.

Paul, as a Roman himself, spoke from the Roman point of view. Though he was a citizen of Tarsus and from that point of view a member of the Greek world, his Roman citizenship overrode his Greek citizenship, and he had beyond all doubt been educated from infancy to understand his position as a Roman.[8] His point of view is clearly and emphatically Roman. Those who talk of Paul as a mere Jew are blinding themselves to his real position and to the character of the Graeco-Roman world in his time.

But Luke's point of view was not the same. Luke is throughout his work a Greek, never a Roman; and his statements must be estimated accordingly. Before criticizing, we must make sure that we understand rightly; and we shall never understand rightly, unless we begin by sympathizing with the writer and the tone of his work.

Luke then speaks of things Roman as they appeared to a Greek. The Greeks never could quite understand Roman matters; even the mysteries of the Roman system of personal names were as puzzling to almost all Greeks as they are to a modern school boy or college student.⁹ Hence, for example, in the remarkable scene at Paphos (Acts 13:9), it is difficult to feel any confidence whether or not Paul disclosed himself to Sergius Paullus in his Roman character. If he did so, it is clear that his Roman name ought to be given. Strictly taken, Luke›s language at this point implies that Paul showed himself only as a Greek traveler and philosopher to the Roman proconsul; and, on the whole, this seems perhaps most probable. But that must be gathered from the career of Paul as a whole; and it would not be safe to infer it from the fact that Luke gives the alternative name in its Greeks not in its Roman form. Paul did not, perhaps, develop his idea of Christianity for the Roman empire quite so early.

Luke, indeed, does not distinctly mark any further stage of development; but to Luke the great antithesis – Gentile and Jew – quite obliterated the lesser distinction between Roman citizen and Roman provincial, when the provincial was a Greek. What power lay in the Roman name, the thorough Greek never comprehended; and hence Luke has never disclosed to us the fact – which is beyond all doubt – that Paul had a Roman name. Had it been clearly present in the consciousness of all modern scholars that Paul must have been either Gaius Julius Paullus or something of that style, many things that have been said would have been better said, or left unsaid. Yet it is as certain as anything can be, that a Roman citizen necessarily had a Roman name, that Paul could not have revealed himself to the magistrates at Philippi or to Claudius Lysias, and that he could not have appealed to the emperor, except by virtue of his Roman name, which he must have stated openly.

Owing to the failure of a Greek to comprehend Roman names and their importance, we have no clear record about this important side of Paul's career. Luke sees him only in two aspects, as "Hebrew or Graeco Roman": he never sees him as "Greek or Roman".[10]

As a preparation for the study of Luke's History, one ought to become familiar with the remains of the Greek used in the cities of the wider Greece,[11] to understand as far as possible the ideas of the people among whom Luke grew up, and to appreciate the way in which they rendered or misrendered Roman things. We shall then begin to appreciate better Luke›s meaning and his standard as a historian. It is true that he regularly uses the popular phraseology, and not the strictly and technically accurate terms for Roman things;[12] but he is decidedly more accurate in essentials than the ordinary Greek, even the official Greek, of the Eastern cities. He never is guilty of the blunders that puzzle the epigraphist in Asian or Galatian inscriptions.

It has often been remarked that Luke wrote for a public ignorant of Palestine, its customs and its language, and familiar with the surroundings of Graeco-Roman life in the great cities of the empire. He explains to his readers Semitic names and terms; he describes the situation of Nazareth and Capernaum as cities of Galilee, of Arimathea as a city of the Jews, of the country of the Gadarenes as over against Galilee, and he even tells the distance of the Mount of Olives and of Emmaus from Jerusalem.

Now contrast with these explanations the allusions to the cities of the Greek and Italian lands. The fact that Syracuse and Puteoli and Rhegium are named without any geographical explanation might perhaps be explained from their fame and importance. Syracuse was one of the greatest Greek cities; Puteoli was the great harbor for passengers by the sea voyage to Rome from the East; and Rhegium was situated at a very striking point on the voyage. Similarly, while he explains the position of Philippi and Perga, Myra and Lystra, he assumes that the situation of Athens, of Corinth, and of Ephesus is familiar to his readers. He thinks that the coasts of the Aegean Sea need no explanation, or that the general character of the voyage sufficiently explains the position of Troas, Cos, Miletus, Caesarea and Ptolemais. The relation of Cenchreae to Corinth (Acts 18:18) is also taken as familiar. But the most striking case occurs as the travelers approach Rome. The author assumes that the Market of Appius and the Three Taverns are familiar points on the road, which Paul must traverse between Puteoli and Rome. Instead of telling their distance from Rome, he uses them as actual measures of distance to show how far the brethren came forth from Rome to welcome Paul.

Too much stress should not be laid on reasoning so slight as this. There is not enough of evidence to justify full confidence. But, so far as it goes, it suggests that Luke wrote for an audience which knew the environs of Rome and Corinth far more intimately than the country round Jerusalem and the Sea of Galilee. And, on the whole, it is on the great lines of communication leading from Syria and Asia to Rome that most knowledge is assumed.

Further, Luke sometimes adapts incidents to the comprehension of his readers by expressing them in terms which, though not a literal description of the original facts, approximate to the general sense and are more readily intelligible to the Western reader. An excellent example of this is found in Luke 5:17-20, as compared with Mark 2:1-4.

MARK 2:1-4	LUKE 5:17-20
And when he entered again into Capernaum after some days, it was noised that he was in the house. And many were gathered together, so that there was no longer room for them, no, not even about the door · and he spake the word unto them. And they come, bringing unto him a man sick of the palsy, borne of four. And when they could not come nigh unto him for the crowd, they uncovered the roof where he was[13] and when they had broken it up, they let down the bed whereon the sick of the palsy lay.	And it came to pass on one of those days, that he was teaching; and there were Pharisees and doctors of the law sitting by, which were come out of every village of Galilee and Judea and Jerusalem: and the power of the Lord was with him to heal. And behold, men bring on a bed a man that was palsied' and they sought to bring him in, and to lay him before him. And not finding by what way they might bring him in because of the multitude, they went up to the house-top, and let him down through the tiles with his couch into the midst before Jesus.

Here it is obvious that Mark gives the incident in the more exact way. The house was a humble erection, with a flat roof of earth or other material, which was easily destroyed and as easily replaced. The bearers

PART I. Importance of the Problem

took advantage of this; mounting on the roof, they broke it up, and let down the couch through the hole which they thus made.

A modern writer might have explained all this to his readers. But Luke, although he interprets a single Semitic word occasionally, would not spare time and space enough for a more elaborate description of details, which were, in his estimation, unimportant. His readers were familiar with a different kind of house, covered with tiles, and having a hole (*impluvium*) in the roof of the principal chamber (*atrium*), where the company would be assembled. To turn aside from his proper subject and describe differences of architecture would have distracted attention from the really important facts. As has been often pointed out,[14] Luke never describes such features, but leaves his readers to imagine for themselves from their own knowledge the surroundings amid which his story was enacted.

Accordingly, he preserves all the essential features – the dense crowd preventing access to the Master by the proper approach the taking of the bed with the sick man in it up on the roof the letting down of the bed through the roof before the Savior's eyes. But he does not tell that the bearers broke a hole through the roof. A tiled roof, such as his readers were accustomed to, is strong; a hole cannot easily be made through it; and when it is broken, it is a long and expensive operation to repair it. It would seem unnatural that a hole should be violently made in such a roof; and Luke leaves his readers to apply their own knowledge, and to understand that the bearers let the man on his couch down through (the opening in) the tiles.

Matthew, again, regards all these details about the manner of bringing the man as unimportant, and omits them. Corresponding to Mark 2:2-4 and Luke 5:18, 19, he has only these words, 9:2:" And behold they brought him a man sick of the palsy, lying on a bed". It was only the words and acts of the Master that he considered worthy of space. Luke and Mark and Matthew all say that Jesus, "seeing their faith," told the man that his sins were forgiven. He saw that the man had the same "faith able to receive cure and salvation" as the lame man at Lystra, Acts 14. But Luke and Mark explain how the special circumstances made evident the faith of the bearers and the man, while Matthew leaves the reader to gather from Jesus' words, that he saw some special evidence of faith in the case before him, Matthew relates the story as one long familiar; and it would not be thoroughly intelligible to us without the proof of eager faith which Luke and Mark relate. The latter stand on an earlier stage than Matthew.

We notice that Luke's account here is not suited to a Greek house, but only to a Roman house. The Greek house was of totally different construction from the Roman; and, if Luke had been writing primarily for a public resident in the great Greek cities of the Aegean lands, he would probably have either related the incident in its original Palestinian form, or imparted to it a turn that would suit the style of house usual in those cities. It happens, fortunately, that we can illustrate and prove this point by a series of analogous cases.

The Roman comic dramatists, Plautus and Terence, adapted Greek plays to the Roman stage, modifying the plot and incidents in some respects to suit the tastes and the knowledge of a Roman audience. When some incident in the Greek play turned on a peculiarity in the structure of a Greek house, the Roman playwright often modified the facts, so as to suit the style of house that was familiar to his audience. Thus, a Greek dramatist wrote a play called "The Braggart," in which the relation between two lovers is discovered by a slave resident in the neighboring house. In adapting this play, Plautus describes this discovery in the form that the slave, pursuing an ape which had escaped from his master's house, clambered over the roof of the *atrium* of his neighbor›s house, and in this way was able to look through the hole in the roof or *impluvium* into the *atrium*, and saw the lovers sitting side by side.

As Lorenz has observed,[15] this could not have been the form which the incident had in the original Greek play. The Greek house had no atrium with its impluvium, nor anything corresponding to it. The ordinary house in the Greek cities contained an open court or aula, to which access was gained by a passage leading from the front door. This court was surrounded, sometimes simply by the house walls, sometimes by a narrow stoa or portico,[16] resting on the house walls and supported inside by columns. The covered chambers of the house opened off the back of this court, and the part of the mansion which contained these chambers was usually of one or, at most, two stories and covered by a flat roof. As the houses in these Greek cities were usually built close together, divided from one another by the house wall (which was common to both), it was easy to look from the flat roof (or from the windows of the upper story) of one house into the court of the next; and thus the slave in the Greek play saw the lovers in the *aula* of the neighboring house. In this same way Thekla at Iconium sat at a window in the house of her mother Theokleia, and heard Paul preaching in the court of the house of Onesiphorus, her neighbor. See note 2 at the end of this chapter.

Luke uses even the Roman form of expression. The regular term for "the roof" (regarded from the outside) was in Latin "the tiles";[17] but in Greek the collective singular form «the tiling» was used.[18] Luke speaks after the Roman fashion, and says that they let the sick man down «through the tiles» (διὰ τῶν κεράμων). by which he implies the roof of Roman style. In a similar way, Terence in the *Phormio*, 707, speaks of a snake as having "fallen from the tiles (*i.e.*, the roof) through the impluvium," expressing the same meaning in a fuller way.

In a review in the *Theologische Litteraturzeitung,* 1897, p. 534, Dr. Johannes Weiss says: «When Mark writes they uncovered the roof, and when they had broken it up, they let down the bed, ‹ but Luke on the other hand says they let him down through the tiles, ‹ the former thinks of the Palestinian style of building, while the latter thinks of the roof of the Graeco-Roman house». This expresses practically the same view which has been advocated in the preceding pages, but the word Graeco-Roman seems to require modification. Luke writes with a view to the Roman house alone; and his language would not suit the Greek style of house.

Luke must have adapted his expression to suit either a circle of readers, or more probably the single reader, Theophilus, for whose instruction he composed his History; and, in giving to his narrative the form seen in 5:20, he evidently felt that Theophilus was used to the Roman and not the Greek house architecture. Taking this in conjunction with the use made of the Market of Appius and the Three Taverns, we find a distinct probability that Theophilus was a citizen of Rome.

Moreover, Theophilus is addressed by an epithet,[19] which, under the empire, was peculiarly appropriated to Romans of high rank, and which became during the second century a technical title indicating equestrian (as distinguished from senatorial) rank. Examples are numerous in the Imperial Greek inscriptions; and those who have made themselves familiar with the usages of Roman and provincial life under the empire, will recognize the high probability that Luke uses this adjective in 1:4, as in every other place (Acts 23:26, 24:3 and 26:25) [20] to indicate the official (probably equestrian) rank of the person to whom he applies it.

Luke, then, was adapting the form of his narrative either to a single Roman or to a Roman circle of readers. The frequency and emphasis with which he mentions matters that are specifically Roman must impress every reader.

In regard to Roman officials of high rank, the favorable judgment which they always pass on Christ and on his followers is so marked a feature of Luke's work, that it must have been prominent before his mind.

Luke mentions formally the charge which the Jews vainly made, that Jesus had been guilty of disloyalty and treason against the Roman emperor, 23:2. John mentions it very informally (John 18:30). [21] Matthew and Mark are silent about the nature of the charge. Luke records the thrice repeated judgment of Pilate acquitting Jesus of all fault before the Roman law; John mentions the acquittal once in similar terms; Matthew represents Pilate as disclaiming all responsibility for his death, but not as formally pronouncing him innocent of all fault.

In Luke's Second Book this feature is still more marked. The Imperial officers stand between Paul and the Jews to save him from them. The Proconsul of Cyprus was almost converted to Christianity. The Proconsul of Achaia dismissed the Jews' case against him as groundless before the law. Festus, the Procurator of Palestine, found in Paul nothing worthy of death – he had difficulty in discovering any definite charge against him, which he could report in sending him up to the supreme court of the empire. Even Felix, another Procurator, one of the worst of Roman officials, was affected by Paul's teaching, and to some extent protected him, and did not condemn him, though to please the Jews he left him in prison.

Among inferior Roman officials, Claudius Lysias, Julius, Cornelius, even the jailer in the colony of Philippi, were friendly to the Christians, or actually joined them. In the few cases in which the magistrates of a Roman colony took action against Paul, their action is shown to have been in error (as at Philippi), or is passed over in silence and the blame is laid on the jealousy and hatred of the Jews (as at Pisidian Antioch and Lystra). The praetors of Philippi scourged Paul, but they apologized, and confessed they had been in the wrong. The magistrates of the Greek cities, like Iconium, Thessalonica and Athens, were far more severe against Paul than those of Roman colonies.[22]

Even the publicans, those hated instruments of a taxation after the Jewish and Romanising style, are far more kindly treated by Luke than by Matthew or Mark. Compare, for example, the "publicans and sinners" in the house of Levi or Matthew. Both Mark and Matthew designate the company by this name; but Luke calls them "publicans and others," and confines the more opprobrious phrase to the mouth of the scribes (Matthew 9:10; Mark 2:15; Luke 5:29, cp. 7:34). Luke alone sets the publican and the Pharisee over against one another as good and bad types, 18:10. It is true that several sayings of Christ in favor of publicans are given also by Matthew and Mark; they were too characteristic to be omitted; but Luke has more of them.

It is not unconnected with this character in his work that Luke records with special interest the acts and words of Christ implying that the Gospel was as open to the Gentiles as to the Jews. Similar examples are found in all the Gospels, because no one who gave a fair account of the teaching of Christ could omit them; but in Luke they are more numerous and more emphatic.[23]

It has been, however, pointed out, as a proof that such examples cannot be relied on, that Luke omits entirely the story of the Savior's visit to Phoenicia, including the case of the Syrophoenician woman whose great faith was commended. But in that story occurs the saying, "I was not sent but unto the lost sheep of the house of Israel," Matthew 15:24; and in view of such sayings as Luke – and Luke alone – records in 4:25-27 (see Luke 24:47 paralleled by Matthew 28:19, and Mark 16:15), the historian might doubt whether the incident was not likely to give a mistaken impression of the Savior's mission. As to the passing in silence over a visit to Phoenicia, it is pointed out below,[24] that Luke deliberately refrains from describing the journeys and movements of Christ.

It is, therefore, plain on the face of Luke's History, that he has taken pains to connect his narrative with the general history of the empire, and that he has noted with special care the relations between the new religion and the Roman state or its officials. Elsewhere I have tried to show that Luke thought of his work, from one point of view, as "an appeal to the truth of history against the immoral and ruinous policy of the reigning emperor; a temperate and solemn record by one who had played a great part in them of the real facts regarding the formation of the Church, its steady and unswerving loyalty in the past, its firm resolve to accept the existing Imperial government, its friendly reception by many Romans, and its triumphant vindication in the first great trial at Rome. The book was the work of one who had been trained by Paul to look forward to Christianity becoming the religion of the empire and of the world, who regarded Christianity as destined not to destroy but to recreate the empire.[25]

In such circumstances it is obvious that the historian was bound to be specially careful that his references to matters of Roman history, and especially his first reference – the subject of this study – were accurate. But the accusation which we have to meet is that it grossly misrepresented the character of Roman procedure, and was inaccurate in fact. If the accusation is right, any Roman citizen who possessed even a small knowledge of the facts of administration must have seen the gross inaccuracy at a glance. How, then, does it happen that, while the circumstances of the birth of Christ were closely scrutinized by the opponents of Christianity and subjected to much misrepresentation and many charges of falsification, no one in Roman times seems ever to have discovered the inaccuracies which many modern inquirers imagine to themselves?

PART I. Importance of the Problem

NOTE 1

Professor Blass in his welcome book, *Philology of the Gospels*, 1898, p. 19, declares that the epithet κράτιστος in Luke›s language, had no such force as we find in it, but was merely «the ordinary one in epistolary and oratorical style, when the person addressed was in a somewhat exalted position». As examples, he quotes Paul›s address to Felix and Festus, who were both Roman officials of equestrian rank! These are two of the many instances on which the proof rests that the title was peculiarly appropriated at that period to Romans of rank. The same scholar refers, further, to the examples quoted by Otto in his edition of the *Epistle to Diognetus,* p. 79 ff. (53 ff.). I cannot consult this book, but Otto considers that Diognetus was the philosopher, the friend and teacher of Marcus Aurelius, and the emperor might well raise his teacher to equestrian rank, as Septimius Severus raised Antipater, the teacher of his sons, to the much higher dignity of the consulship; and, if Otto›s identification be accepted, we may regard the epithet as a proof that Diognetus was honored by his imperial pupil Galen[26] addresses κράτιστε Βάσσε, also a Roman of rank. Longinus addresses Postumius Terentianus, Plutarch speaks of Fundanus, and Artemidorus of Cassius Maximus by the same epithet, in all cases undoubtedly employing it in the technical imperial sense. Epaphroditus, to whom Josephus dedicated his *Jewish Antiquities and Life*, is a more doubtful case; but the dedication implies that he was a man of influence in Rome, and though obviously a freedman (on account of his name), he probably had been honored with equestrian rank by his imperial patron. The Aphrodisius whom Galen addresses as κράτιστε and φίλτατε in his *Prognost.* (Kuhn, vol. 19), is also uncertain; Galen, however, lived amid high society in Rome.

I have always conceded that Greeks were not invariably accurate in using Latin titles and technical terms, such as *optimus* (translated κράτιστος); but the above examples show how often the technical and accurate sense is found in Greek. But Professor Blass has his mind so fixed on Greek literature, of which he is one of the first exponents in Europe, that he sometimes omits to notice Roman facts.

The usage in Theophrastus, of course, lies apart from our subject and belongs to an earlier period of society. Even Horace's *optimus*, used of Octavius and Quinctius, is pre-imperial, though both men were persons of rank in Rome, and therefore conform to our rule.

NOTE 2

In the *Acta* of Paul and Thekla Paul was preaching in the house of Onesiphorus ἐν μέσῳ τῆς ἐκκλησίας (or without the last two words): is the last word a later alteration of the original αὐλῆς? In the Armenian version Paul preached in the house of Onesiphorus in a great assembly, and Thekla sat at a window which was close to their roof.

---

[8] Much might be said on this subject; but it belongs to a study of Paul›s life, and the proofs are found at intervals throughout his career. The subject is touched upon several times in *St. Paul the Traveller*, e.g., pp. 30 f., 225, 315.

[9] The difficulty of being accurate about Roman personal names might be illustrated plentifully even from the books of distinguished modern classical scholars, an unpleasant topic from which I refrain.

[10] I should now be inclined to modify lines 6, 12, 16 of *St. Paul the Traveller*, p. 83, so as to eliminate the word «Roman». Except in those 143 lines, the scene is there described on Paul's Greek side, as I think is right.

[11] Canon Hicks in *Classical Review*, 1887, pp. 4, 42; Deissmann, *Bibelstudien*, 1895, and *Neue Bibelstudien*, 1897. See also *Expository Times*, Oct., 1898, p. 9.

[12] *St. Paul the Traveller*, pp. 30 f., 111, 135, 255, etc.

[13] Literally, «they unroofed the roof».

[14] e.g., *St. Paul the Traveller*, p. 17.

[15] See the introduction to his edition of Plautus, *Miles Gloriosus*, p. 11.

[16] In that case the court was called *peristylium*.

[17] *Tegulæ*: see Brix's note on Plautus, *Miles Gloriosus*, 156.

[18] κέραμος: see Pollux, 7., 162; Aristophanes, *Clouds*, 1127; Thucydides, 2., 4, etc.

[19] κράτιστος See Note 1 at the end of chapter 3.

[20] See Note 1 at end of chapter 3.

[21] «If this man were not an evildoer, we should not have delivered him up unto thee».

[22] The subject of this paragraph is more fully treated in *St. Paul the Traveller*, p. 304 ff.

[23] Alford quotes 4:25-27, 9:52-56, 10:33, 15:11 ff., 17:16-18, 18:10 ff., 19:5,9.

[24] See Chapter 10 ff.

[25] *St. Paul the Traveller*, p. 309 f.

[26] *De libr. suis* (Kuhn, vol. 19.).

Chapter 4.
IMPORTANCE IN LUKE'S HISTORY OF THE STORY OF THE BIRTH OF CHRIST

IT needs no proof that Luke attached the highest importance to this part of his narrative. That Jesus was indicated from the beginning as the Messiah – though not a necessary part of his life and work, and wholly omitted by Mark and only briefly indicated in mystical language by John – was a highly interesting and important fact in itself, and could not fail to impress the historian. The elaboration and detail of the first two chapters of the Gospel form a sufficient proof that Luke recognized the importance of the central incident in them.

Further, the author must have regarded this part of his work with special interest, and been impelled to work it up with peculiar care, on account of the authority on which it rested; and he takes some pains to show his reader what was the authority.

The beautifully told story of Luke 1, 2, is an episode of family history of the most private character. The facts could be known only to a very small number of persons. If Luke had the slightest trace of historical instinct, he must have satisfied himself that the narrative which he gives rested on the evidence of one of the few persons to whom the facts could be known. It is not in keeping with the ancient style that he should formally name his authority; but he does not leave it doubtful whose authority he believed himself to have. "His mother kept all these sayings hid in her heart;" "Mary kept all these sayings, pondering them in her heart;" (Luke 2:19 and 51) those two sentences would be sufficient. The historian who wrote like that believed that he had the authority of the Mother herself.

But those two sentences are not the only indications of the source whence Luke believed his information to come. Some facts intimately concerning Elizabeth are mentioned in 1:24 and 41; and the narrative carefully explains how these facts became known to Mary, 1:36 and 41 she had been told. But it is never stated that facts intimately concerning Mary were mentioned by her to Elizabeth. The narrative has the form which is natural only if Mary is understood to be the authority throughout: she simply states what concerned herself, while, in what concerned Elizabeth, she not merely states the facts, but also explains that she has first-hand authority.

Moreover, what concerned Mary is expressly said to have remained secret, known to herself alone and pondered over in her own heart. It would be a contradiction that this secret of her heart should be the property of others to tell about her. The historian, by emphasizing the silence and secrecy in which she treasured up the facts, gives the reader to understand that she is the authority.

It is a different thing when we read, 1:65 f., "these sayings were noised abroad throughout all the hill country of Judea. And all that heard them laid them up in their hearts, saying, *What then shall this child be?*" There a subject of notoriety, which deeply impressed the whole district, is referred to. What is known to many is no secret, and in fact is expressly said to have been a topic of conversation through the country.

The people in the hill country of Judea knew about the marvelous circumstances of John's birth, and talked about it, and wondered. But at Nazareth nothing was generally known. Jesus had been born far away. His parents brought him to Nazareth after some time had elapsed. Even after Herod's death his shadow lay heavy on the land; and the parents, being subjects of his son Antipas, were not likely to talk to their neighbors about the old king's relations to the child and about the prophecies of Simeon and Anna apart from the consideration that the whole subject must have seemed too sacred for gossip. Mary did not herself comprehend the things that had occurred. She kept them hid in her heart, and apparently did not even tell her husband what was in her mind. This child was not to be an unalloyed delight either to her country or herself; he was "set for the falling and rising up of many in Israel, and for a sign which is spoken against"; and for herself, "a sword should pierce through her own soul". It was a dread and vague future about which she pondered in the depths of her own mind, as "the child grew and waxed strong, filled with wisdom". In that marvelous picture, sketched in such simple and brief terms, only he that deliberately shuts his mind against all literary feeling can fail to catch the tone of a mother's heart.

In the description of the early days of John and of Jesus the reader notices the woman's and the mother's feeling, watching the growth of the two children, to whom and through whom so much had been promised. As to John, "the child grew and waxed strong and was in the wilderness (of Judah, the remote country of his birth) till the day of his showing unto Israel". But about her own son there is an added touch of warmth, "the child grew and waxed strong, filled with wisdom; and the grace of God was upon him" (Luke 1:80, 2:40).

No one who judges on the ordinary canons of criticism which govern the interpretation of ancient literature, can doubt that it is through design, and not by accident, that there occur in the opening chapters of Luke's History all these little touches, indicating so delicately and so skillfully what authority he had to depend upon in the beginning of his narrative. This is specially clear when we remember the declaration made by the author in his preface, that he had investigated from their origin the facts which he is going to narrate. After such a preface, and with all the indications in the narrative, it is plain that the historian either believed his statements to be based on the authority of the Virgin Mary herself, or has deliberately tried to create a false impression that such was the case. Is it a rational supposition, is it psychologically possible, that any man who was impressed with the sacredness of the subject which he is treating should intentionally found his narrative upon such a falsehood as this would be?

Understanding that Mary herself is the authority to whom Luke appeals, we find that the passage becomes clearer, both as to what it states and what it omits.

The origin of the narrative may possibly explain why Luke and Matthew give such different accounts of the circumstances of the birth of Christ. Matthew gives the public account, that which was generally known during the Savior's life and after his death; and popular belief has always some tendency to transform and adapt to moral purposes facts that are much talked about. Luke gives from knowledge gained within the family an account of facts known only to the family, and in part to the Mother alone.

It is most probable that Luke had heard the story which Matthew gives, and it would have been easy to fit this into his own narrative without disturbing either account. But they did not rest on equal authority; and Luke would not mix the two. What he had got was an account of the miraculous birth and of the circumstances which had most deeply impressed the Mother's mind with regard to the origin and mission of her Child, while it was rather the relations of the Child to the old king that had impressed themselves on the imagination of his followers. In them Matthew read a fulfillment of prophecies about the Messiah. But they had not similarly affected Mary's mind, and they were not among the facts which she pondered over in her heart as pledges of the great future that lay before this little Child.

Luke therefore confined himself to what he had on the highest authority. So much he states in full detail; and the rest of the first twelve years of Jesus' life he sums up in the brief expression, 2:40: "He was filled with wisdom and the grace of God was upon him". Then came a remarkable instance of the young Boy's awakening consciousness of his own mission. He had been brought up by his Mother to think of Joseph as his father; but suddenly he declared to her that his Father's business lay in a different direction. Here, again, there was something for the Mother's heart to ponder over, while her Son went on once more in the natural development of a boy, "increasing in wisdom and stature and in favor with God and man".

We can argue, then, with perfect confidence that Luke did not take the narrative of the birth and childhood of Christ from mere current talk and general belief: he had it in a form for which Mary herself was in his opinion the responsible authority. What, then, was this form? It must have been either written narrative or oral communication.

If it were written, the writer must have been either Mary herself or some one who recorded her story so carefully and faithfully as to leave full expression to Mary's own feelings.

PART I. Importance of the Problem

That Mary herself wrote it seems highly improbable. We should not expect that she had the literary interest or skill which might lead her to wish to perpetuate the facts in her own formal narrative: it is more probable, considering the circumstances of her position in youth, that she would lack the power of setting down a story in written expression with such rare art as to have the appearance of being perfectly natural, even though she would be able to tell it well orally in simple, natural, unstudied words. Moreover, it seems improbable that she should desire of her own self to make public the facts which she had kept so long hid in her heart. It is more natural to think that she hardly ever spoke of them, except to the rare individuals whose sympathy drew her on. The language, too, has a tone and character that do not suggest a formal autobiographical narrative. It seems, if I may venture to express my individual opinion, to be one of those which lose from being recited in public; it is one to be read alone or in the company of some perfectly sympathetic person, but which suffers from the presence of any one who is not in perfect sympathy. It expresses the heart of Mary; but in the form in which it was expressed to a sympathetic heart, and not as prepared for publication.

It is more easily conceivable that some third person, intimate with Mary and recognizing the importance of having an authoritative narrative of these events, should have given literary form to an account coming direct from her own lips. But this account must have been either a part of a complete life of Christ one of those which Luke refers to in his preface, 1:1, "repeated[27] according as they who were from the beginning eyewitnesses or the word delivered the tradition» – or an independent narrative, ranking with the authority of origin from Mary, and describing just so much as she was best able to tell.

The existence of such an independent narrative, and the utter oblivion into which it fell, if it ever existed, seem alike most improbable. Moreover, suppose, for example, the author who gave it literary form to have been John, in whose house she lived from the crucifixion till her death, we must suppose that her words have passed through the modifying influence of John's mind; thereafter John's words have passed through the modifying influence of Luke's mind; and yet, after all this, they continue to show clear and fresh the marks of their origin. The narrative seems not to have passed through so many stages.

Further, the earliest followers of Christ seem to have been so entirely occupied with his engrossing personality that they thought little or not at all about his Mother. She hardly appears in three of the four Gospels.

Matthew tells the story of the birth of her son in such a way that Joseph is the prominent person, and Mary a mere adjunct. On the few occasions on which she appears directly or indirectly, in Matthew and in Mark "there is a sound of reproof in the words" which Christ uses to her or of her: Matthew 12:46, 13:56 f., Mark 3:31 ff., Matthew 6:3 f. They do not mention her among the women who watched in sorrow at the crucifixion. It has been suggested that they omitted her name in this scene, because it was obvious that she would be there; but no ordinary reader of these two Gospels would gather from them that this was obvious.

The tone which John's references to her convey depends mainly on the interpretation of John 2:4. There the Savior says to her, according to the almost universal interpretation, "Woman, what have I to do with thee?" (τί ἐμοὶ καὶ σοί, γύναι) in a tone of reproof and almost (it might appear) of dislike, as is seen in the illustrative cases which are usually quoted Matthew 17:19, 2 Samuel 16:10, 1 Kings 17:18, 2 Chronicles 35:21 and Judges 11:12. Is this the tone of the only information that John gives about the woman who lived in his house from the day of the crucifixion till her death? The more one thinks of it, the more one hopes that Luther was right when he desired to take the meaning, "what is that to me and to thee?"[28] The old Egyptian poet of the fourth or fifth century, Nonnus, understood the words in that way, for he slightly varies them in his metrical paraphrase, reading

τί ἐμοί, γύναι, ἠὲ σοὶ αὐτῇ;

Professor Blass considers that Nonnus had before him a MS. of the fourth Gospel in which ἠ was read where all now existing MSS. have καὶ, and argues that we should replace ἠ in the text. We should rather suppose that Nonnus (and probably the whole Asian circle for whom the fourth Gospel was primarily intended) understood the accepted text in the same sense as Luther advocated.

In all that part of Luke's History which is parallel with the common tradition in Matthew and Mark, he mentions Mary only in the same way as they do, and gives no more information about her than they have; and like them, he does not mention her presence at the crucifixion. The only additional allusion to her that he gives in the main body of his narrative, is contained in the words of an unnamed woman, blessing her who had given birth to such a son as Jesus (Luke 11:27) Accordingly, considering the interest which Luke shows in Mary in the beginning of the Gospel, and in Acts 1:14, where she is mentioned as being in steadfast companionship with the Apostles, it seems probable that the written authorities which he had before him told the story of the Savior without referring except in the most casual way to his Mother.

It, therefore, seems unlikely that the first two chapters of Luke depend on an older written narrative. The quality in them is too simple and natural, they give too much of the nature of Mary expressed with the art of Luke, to have passed through the mind of an intermediate writer. And it is difficult to think that any such composition either could have existed in Luke's time, or would have disappeared without leaving a trace behind, if it had existed.

This result is diametrically opposite to the prevailing opinion. It is generally assumed as specially clear, that we have in the narrative of the birth and childhood of Jesus a translation from an Aramaic narrative or from a series of Aramaic narratives. Instead of seeing evidence of Luke's literary power in the variations of style in different parts of his history, many scholars see only evidence of difference in documentary authority. As if the person who wrote the preface 1:1-4 could be blind to the complete change in style between 1:4 and 1:5! Or as if he were unable to put the story into his own Greek, if he desired. It is clear as noon-day that the author deliberately aims at the contrast in style between 1:1-4 and the following verses.

But that there must be a number of separate documents underlying the narrative of 1 and 2, which Luke translated, seems an even more objectionable idea. Because there are three distinct statements about the growth of John, of the infant Jesus, and of the boy Jesus, it is assumed by some writers that these form the conclusions of separate documents. The slight but significant differences between them, in which I see evidence at once of literary art and of the natural motherly feeling of Mary, are treated as being mere tag-ends of separate narratives, which the author of this History had not art enough to hide. He was so incapable of working separate authorities into a unity, that he comes to three separate ends, because he had three separate authorities before him.

"And the child grew and waxed strong in spirit, and was in the deserts till the day of his showing unto Israel," 1:80.

"And the child grew and waxed strong in spirit, filled with wisdom; and the grace of God was upon him," 2:40.

"And Jesus increased in wisdom and stature and in favor with God and man," 2:52.

But, in truth, these three sentences mark three stages in a continuous, unified narrative, written with the finest feeling and art by a single author of the loftiest literary power. They are a quite sufficient proof to one who judges on literary grounds that this is not a composite narrative, but the work of the same writer throughout.

If we are right in this view as to Luke's authority and as to the way in which that authority reached him, *viz.*, by oral communication, it appears that either the Virgin was still living when Luke was in Palestine during the years 57 and 58 – which is quite a possible supposition on the almost universally accepted assumption that she was quite young when Jesus was born – or Luke had conversed with some one very intimate with her, who knew her heart and could give him what was almost as good as firsthand information. Beyond that we cannot safely go; but yet one may venture to state the impression – though it may be generally considered merely fanciful – that the in, termediary, if one existed, is more likely to have been a woman than a man. There is a womanly spirit in the whole narrative, which seems inconsistent with the transmission from man to man,[29] and which, moreover, is an indication of Luke›s character: he had a, marked sympathy with women.

Many other facts in his History show that character. Luke alone mentions the "women which had been healed of evil spirits and infirmities," who "ministered to him of their substance"; and he names them: he was interested in themselves, in their gratitude to Jesus, and in their reason for it (Luke 8:2).

He alone tells of the woman who wet Jesus' feet with her tears, and wiped them with her hair, and kissed them, and anointed them – her to whom her many sins were forgiven, because she loved much. He does not tell her name – was it because she had been a sinner, and he would not chronicle that fact about a definite person? or was his information defective (Luke 7:36)? [30]

He alone tells about the different characters of Martha and Mary of Bethany, though he left much for John to add (Luke 10:38). Matthew and Mark do not mention their names, but allude to Mary in an obscure and almost inaccurate way.

He alone tells of the women of Jerusalem who followed him to his death, bewailing and lamenting. All three synoptics mention the women who had followed Jesus from Galilee, and stood watching the crucifixion afar off, and how some of them watched where he was laid; but Luke alone tells how they went away and prepared spices and ointments (Luke 23:27, 56).

He alone tells of the nameless woman in the crowd who blessed the mother of such a Son as Jesus; possibly one of those to whom Jesus afterwards said: "Blessed are the childless women, in those days that are coming" (Luke 23:29 compare Luke 11:27).

Thus time after time, Luke is our only authority for the service and ministration of women. He had the tender and sympathetic feeling for women which seems to be quite in keeping with his surroundings in Macedonia (where women occupied a place of so much more honor than in Greece proper), and which makes him record so often in his second book the part played by women in the diffusion of the new religion.

In the texture of the two opening chapters we find full justification for the prominence that the preface lays upon this episode; and we conclude that both the personal character of the author and the high authority on which he claims to rest, would prompt him to lavish special loving care on this part of his narrative and to avoid defacing it by a serious blunder. If he made a blunder, as seems generally admitted, that would be a sufficient refutation of the view which I have maintained, that he was a great historian.

NOTE

Probably the most reasonable explanation of the remarkable discrepancies between the four passages – Matthew 26:6-13, Mark 14:3-9, Luke 7:36-50 and John 12:1-9 (cp. 11:2) – is that there were two distinct incidents: one occurred in the house of Simon the Pharisee, and is described by Luke; the other occurred in the house of Martha and Mary at Bethany, and is correctly described by John. Mark, and following him Matthew, mix up the two and describe the incident as occurring at Bethany in the house of Simon the Leper. They, do not name the woman, and they merely say that she poured a box of ointment over the head of Jesus. The attempts to harmonize John with Mark and Matthew fail completely. John, who says that "they made him a supper there and Martha served," obviously places the meal in Martha's house: it seems quite absurd to suppose that she would be serving in the house of Simon. There is an obvious intention on John's part to correct the current account, as seen in Matthew and Mark, and at the same time to illustrate the character of Martha as described by Luke 10:38. Similarly, inasmuch as the current account placed the incident two days before the last supper, John pointedly says it occurred "six days before the Passover".

Probably, Mark originally fell into error from treating two separate incidents, each perhaps only reported in part to him, or in part forgotten by him, as being one and the same incident. From one incident he caught that it had occurred in Bethany, and from another that it occurred in the house of Simon: accordingly he begins "while he was in Bethany in the house of Simon the Leper, as he sat at meat". It must remain uncertain whether Luke's Simon the Pharisee is the same person as Mark's Simon the Leper, or (as seems on the whole more probable) the incident narrated by Luke occurred in the north, near the Sea of Galilee, in the house of Simon the Pharisee, and Mark, connecting the incident at once with Bethany and with Simon, put it in the house of a Simon who lived in Bethany and was or had been a leper. It would be obviously impossible that the feast should be held in the house of one who was a leper; and it seems not very probable that it would be held in his house, if he had ever been a leper.

It must be confessed that there is some temptation to follow the Roman tradition, and treat the Lukan incident as the same with the Johannine. Luke is vague as to the locality, though it is most natural to understand that it occurred in the north. But the decisive argument lies in the moral of the tale. The reason why any incident was remembered by the disciples lay in the lesson which the Master had deduced from it. The features which drew forth the lesson in Luke are precisely those which are most difficult to reconcile with John. To identify the two incidents, it becomes almost necessary to suppose that the features on which the moral hinges are errors on Luke's part. Now I should be quite ready to admit that Luke had made mistakes about various points, provided they were not essential to the moral; but those are precisely the points that are vital, and give vitality to the whole incident. Matthew and Mark are reconciled with John by assuming that they have erred in the accompaniments; but in the vital details they agree with him. To identify Luke and John requires that the vital details are false in one or the other.

The considerations advanced (see chapter 11) ff., if correct, would entirely disprove the identity of the Lukan and the Johannine incident.

---

[27] On the sense of ἀνατάξασθαι see Blass, *Philology of the Gospels*, 1898, p. 14 f.
[28] Dr. E. Nestle in the *Expository Times*, 1898, p. 332.
[29] For Eastern feeling read Lady Duff Gordon›s Letters from Egypt.
[30] 7:36 ff.: See Note at end of chapter.

PART II.
SOLUTION OF THE PROBLEM

Chapter 5.
THE QUESTION AT ISSUE

NEITHER Mark nor John mentions where Jesus was born. Mark 1:9 says: "Jesus came from Nazareth of Galilee and was baptized of John in the Jordan". In John 1:45 Philip speaks of him as "Jesus of Nazareth, the son of Joseph"; and in Acts 10:38 Peter mentions "Jesus of Nazareth".

These expressions obviously do not imply that Mark, or John, or the author of Acts considered Nazareth to be the place of Jesus' birth. They merely show that Nazareth was universally considered to be the abode of his parents, the place which had been his home, coming from which he had appeared before the world. Similarly the expression, "son of Joseph," used by Philip in John 1:45, cannot be taken as indicating John's own opinion, but merely as showing the current belief.

Again, John 7:40, 41, quotes the opinions expressed in Jerusalem about Jesus: some of the multitude said: "This is of a truth the prophet": others said: "This is the Christ": but some said: "What, does the Christ come out of Galilee? Hath not the scripture said that the Christ cometh of the seed of David and from Bethlehem?"

These are the popular sayings, and it is obvious that they are arranged to form a climax; but the last, which is really the strongest recognition of Jesus as the Messiah, gains all the more emphasis because it has the form of an objection to him. He was the Prophet: He was the Christ: He fulfilled all the prophecies about the coming of the Christ. The irony, which makes the objectors unconsciously bear such emphatic witness in his favor, might have been expected to be clear and impressive to every rational mind. But there is no blindness so complete as that of the historical critic with a bad theory to maintain; and the critics of this class actually quote this passage as a proof that John did not believe that Jesus was born in Bethlehem. Would they be consistent, and maintain also that John did not believe him to be of the seed of David, though that was indubitably the accepted doctrine of the early Church, as is attested by Paul, *Romans* 1:3 and *2 Timothy* 2:8, as well as by the Synoptics?

But the two points mentioned by the objectors must go together. They who quote 7:41 as a proof that John did not know the second point must infer also that John did not know the first. Every Christian reader of John's Gospel would recognize the irony involved in the first point, for he knew the doctrine set forth by Paul and the Synoptics. He would therefore necessarily recognize that the second point was also ironical.

Accordingly, every scholar who judges literature on literary grounds will recognize that the writer of the fourth Gospel assumes such perfect familiarity in his readers with the story of the birth in Bethlehem, that not merely must he be ranked among the witnesses to it, but he must have written at a time when this belief was a part of recognized Christian teaching; and it is probable that this will be urged by some scholars as a proof that the fourth Gospel springs from a much later period, after the story as given by Matthew and Luke had had time to become a fundamental part of Church doctrine.

But a remarkable feature in the Gospels, at least of Matthew, Luke and John, is that they assume in their readers such a background of knowledge about the life of the Savior. They are written for the use of persons who were already Christians, and who already had the life of Jesus in their minds as the foundation of their faith. None of the Gospels is intended to be a formal biography: their completeness is moral and spiritual and not historical:"[31] they are, in reality, Gospels. But the facts of the life of Jesus were fundamental in the Gospel, and from that point of view each Gospel had to present a record of facts, actions and words sufficient to bear the structure of faith which had to rest upon it. But John, in particular, assumes that his readers know the facts recorded in the Synoptic Gospels, and his work is an unintelligible phenomenon in literature unless this is recognized.

Now Matthew and Luke agree that Jesus was born in Bethlehem. Matthew 2:6 points out that this place of birth was the fulfillment of the prophecy that the Ruler of Israel was to be born there. Yet they are also fully aware that Jesus was considered by the world to be a native of Nazareth, and that he had been brought up from infancy in that city. Matthew 2:23 again sees in the up-bringing at Nazareth the fulfillment of another prophecy. How, then, do they account for the general oblivion of the real place of birth?

Matthew begins with the birth of Jesus. He tells nothing about any previous connection of his parents with Nazareth; but says that they retired to Nazareth while the Child was still an infant, being in fear of the reigning King of Judea. If Luke's History had not been preserved, it would have been unhesitatingly concluded on the authority of Matthew that the parents of Jesus had never lived at Nazareth until after the birth of the Child. And though Matthew does not explicitly assert that, yet it is hard to think that he could have expressed himself as he has done, if he had known that the parents had their original home in Nazareth.

Luke goes farther back, in accordance with his profession to have studied all things from their origin. He mentions that both Joseph and Mary resided at Nazareth. He tells that they made frequent visits to Jerusalem, and that the mother had relatives there or in the neighborhood; and he explains what was the cause that led them to make a brief visit to Bethlehem at such a moment that Jesus was born there.

Luke does not indeed say explicitly in so many words that the visit was intended to be a mere temporary one; and this has led some commentators to suggest that there may have been an intent on the part of the parents to change their residence to Bethlehem. But the cause stated in John 2:4, 5, implies a mere temporary visit; and the language of Luke 2:39 shows that after the brief visit they returned to their own city, Nazareth, and implies that this had always been their intention.

The occasion of this short visit to Bethlehem is thus described by Luke. In accordance with the orders of the Roman Emperor, Augustus, there was made an enrollment, or numbering, of the population of Herod's kingdom; and this was made according to households and tribal descent and local tribal connection, so that those Hebrews who were not residing in the proper city of their tribe and family were obliged to go to their city in order to be enrolled there.

Further, it seems to be implied that the wife, as well as the head of the house, had to go to the proper city (or for some reason felt it a duty to go), so that the household as a whole might be numbered in the tribal and family center.

Joseph, then, with Mary, his wife, went to his proper city, Bethlehem, to be numbered there among his own people, "because he was of the house and family of David".

It has been maintained by many scholars in modern times that the census is either a fiction or a blunder; that the circumstances connected with it, which Luke relates, are contrary to history; and, in short, that the story is unhistorical and impossible, not in one way merely, but in several. It is asserted as unquestionable that the sole germ out of which the story has developed is the fact, recorded by Josephus, that about AD. 6-7 there was made a census and valuation of Palestine, the first and the only one which the Romans held in that country; and that Luke has transferred this census, with the officer, Quirinius, who made it, to a different period about nine or twelve years earlier, when it was for various reasons impossible that any census could have occurred.

It has been urged with triumphant certainty as established on incontrovertible evidence that the whole story of chapter 2, with all its pathetic and romantic incidents, is a mere fiction, destitute of even as much historical foundation as most historical novels possess. It is asserted as a demonstrated truth that the story contradicts the established facts of contemporary history; and that any one who accepts the ordinary canons of historical reasoning must relegate the whole tale of the birth of Christ to the realm of imaginative fiction. Nor is it only the extreme school of critics that reject the tale as an invention. Many of those scholars who thoroughly accept the trust-worthiness of the Gospel narrative as a whole abandon the attempt to defend this incident, and either pass by on the other side, or frankly admit that it is at least in part erroneous, a mixture of *Dichtung und Wahrheit.*

Against the trustworthiness of this narrative the following are the main lines of argument: –

1. It is declared to be a demonstrated fact that Augustus never ordered any general "Enrollment," or census, to be made of the whole Roman world. Gardthausen, the latest historian of Augustus, speaks most emphatically on this point. He goes even so far as to declare that it is inconsistent with Augustus's aims to attribute to him any such intention: he quotes the words of Luke, and then adds that, for the emperor's plans, a general census of the empire was neither necessary nor suitable.[32]

The eminent German scholar here displays a familiarity with Augustus's intentions and the limits of his aims, which is quite unjustified by the scanty evidence accessible to us. Such assumption of the right to pronounce negative judgments is not the spirit in which the history of Augustus ought to be written, and such a wild statement as this shows a momentary loss of the historic instinct, which enables a writer to distinguish between legitimate inference and loose imagination. It is one of the places in Gardthausen's work where a regret rises strong in every reader's mind that Mommsen[33] has never found opportunity to write the history of that period.

In truth, the distinguished historian of Augustus was not justified in asserting more than that no evidence was known to him corroborating Luke's statement as to Augustus's intentions. It will be my aim to show that evidence was in existence, apparently unknown to Gardthausen, which affords some confirmation of Luke's assertion; and establishes it, when Luke's words are properly translated, on a basis of high historical probability.

2. Even if Augustus had ordered a census to be made of the whole empire, it is maintained that such a census would not have extended to Palestine, which was an independent kingdom and not subject to the orders of Augustus.

There is a mixture of truth and error in this line of argument. It will be our aim to demonstrate that, while the application of the Roman census by Roman officials to Herod's kingdom could not be accepted as credible, yet Luke does not speak of any such application. The argument is founded on a false interpretation. Luke nowhere asserts or

PART II. Solution of the Problem

implies that the census was made by a Roman official. He states that the birth of Jesus occurred in the days of Herod the King of Judea, and in the country over which that king ruled: compare 1:5 and 2:4. He merely mentions the Roman officer, Quirinius, for purposes of dating according to the ancient style, employed generally before eras and numbering of years had come into literary use, just as he mentions various kings and priests in 3:1, 2 for the same purpose. He assumes that his readers would appreciate the fact that the census in the territory of King Herod was conducted under the immediate orders of the king himself.

Further, Luke certainly understands that Herod's kingdom was a part of the Roman world, and that Herod was bound to obey orders issued by Augustus in respect of numbering the population of the Roman world.

We shall have to show – what no one except a theological critic with a theory to maintain would dream of denying – that Herod's kingdom was a part of the Roman world; that it was not independent, but ought rather to be styled a "dependent state"; and that any tendency on the part of such dependent kings to disregard their duty of submission to the general principles of Roman policy was sharply repressed by the emperors.

3. Even if a census had been held in Palestine, it is asserted that there would have been no necessity for Joseph and Mary to go up from Nazareth to the city of Bethlehem, inasmuch as a Roman census would be made according to the existing political and social facts, and would not require that persons should be enrolled according to their place of birth or origin. The Roman method necessarily was to count the population according to their actual residence. It is, however, an essential point in Luke's story, that it should explain how the son of a resident in Nazareth came to be born in Bethlehem, and thus fulfilled the prophecy that the Messiah was to be born in that city. Hence it is contended that Luke's fiction is doubly erroneous, for even if it were true it would not lead to that journey, which is the critical point in the history.

There can be no doubt that in the Roman census the existing facts were recorded, and that any disturbance of the existing distribution of population would defeat the purpose and impair the value of the census. Therefore, if the census which Luke had in mind were one carried out purely after the Roman method, it would not furnish the explanation which is the prime reason for mentioning the census. That must be freely conceded.

But, far from asserting that this census was carried out strictly after the Roman method, Luke explains at the outset that it was made on a different principle, not merely by households (as the Roman method[34] required), but also at the same time according to descent and stock, that is by tribes. It will be our aim to show why this modification of the Roman method was necessary for Herod in his peculiar position: he disguised the Roman and foreign character by the additional requirement that the census should be tribal and thus less alien to the national feeling.

4. It is maintained that no census was ever held in Judea until AD. 6-7, on the ground that that "great census" (Acts 5:37) is described by Josephus as something novel and unheard of, rousing popular indignation and rebellion on that account.

We freely concede that the attempts which have been made to find in Josephus any allusion to an earlier census held under Herod have failed. They have been directed on the wrong lines they have been made with a view to discover signs of such a knowledge of the finances of Palestine as would imply a formal Roman census and valuation made under Herod.

We also fully acknowledge that the earliest census and valuation of property made after the Roman fashion in Palestine took place, as Josephus says, in AD. 7. It is a necessary part of our case that a totally new departure was made in that year; and that the novel, unheard-of, and anti-national proceeding roused indignation and rebellion. In all that Josephus is thoroughly right. But the census of Herod was tribal and Hebraic, not anti-national. It was wholly and utterly unconnected with any scheme of Roman taxation; and it was conducted by Herod on strictly tribal methods. It roused little indignation and no rebellion; and therefore gave no reason for Josephus to notice it.

PART II. Solution of the Problem

It is plain too how great an extent these four arguments against the "Enrollment" hang together, and depend on a false character ascribed to the operation. When Luke's narrative is looked at from the proper point of view by the true historical and sympathetic judgment, with the intention, not of picking all possible faults, but of understanding in the best light the testimony which he gives, we shall see that his evidence explains satisfactorily a peculiarly obscure episode in Roman provincial history. And we shall find that in one more case the progress of discovery in Egypt has set in a new light the problems that seemed insoluble to our predecessors, and made perfectly clear what was obscure to them.

In addition to these four closely connected arguments, another of a different character is advanced.

5. It is affirmed that Quirinius never governed Syria during the life of Herod, for Herod died in 4 BC. and Quirinius was governor of Syria later than 3 BC. and probably in 2 or 1 BC. Therefore a census taken in the time of Quirinius could not be associated with the birth of a child "in the days of Herod, King of Judea".

The conclusion of Mommsen, of Borghesi, and of de Rossi, that Quirinius governed Syria twice, has been generally accepted by modern scholars. Quirinius went to govern Syria for the second time in AD. 6. The proof that his first governorship of Syria fell as late as the year 2 or 1 BC. is incomplete, depending on an estimate of probabilities; and it is founded on the assumption that a statement made by Suetonius is inaccurate. We shall try to show that the decided balance of probabilities is in favor of his having held command in Syria before Herod died. In the present defective state of the evidence, one cannot go further than a probable statement.

The propositions which we seek to defend are only probable. The evidence is too scanty to demonstrate any of them in such a perfectly conclusive fashion that the most prejudiced minds must be convinced. But how many of the "facts" of ancient history are demonstrated beyond all reach of cavil and dissension? Every one who has studied the foundations of ancient history knows that most of our knowledge is founded on a balance of evidence, often a very delicate balance; and, if there were any strong motive to make it worth while fighting the case, almost any detail in ancient history can be called in question. What I am concerned to maintain is that all our positions are the most probable issue of the scanty evidence, and that some of them rest on testimony, outside of Luke's writings, which in ordinary historical criticism is reckoned sufficient justification, while the others are in themselves quite natural, and there is practically no evidence against them, so that Luke's authority should be reckoned as sufficient to establish them.

The possible views with regard to the present question seem to reduce themselves to three: –

1. The story of the birth of Christ, as given by Luke, is so suspicious and encumbered with so many difficulties that it is as a whole incredible.
2. The story is true.
3. The main part of the story is true, but the reference to Quirinius is wrong, and the incident occurred ten to fourteen years before his census. It is possible to cut out the verse about Quirinius, which is a mere date added by Luke, and leave the story otherwise complete; but all the rest hangs together, and if one detail be false, everything is affected.

As to the third alternative, besides the general considerations already urged, see to what a dilemma it reduces its supporters! They acknowledge that the date is added in error by Luke. The rest they hold to be true, because Luke learned it from some other authority not so inaccurate as himself. After discrediting Luke, they proceed to accept everything that is most difficult to believe in his History. But, when the channel through which the story reaches us is unworthy of belief, everything that comes through the channel is discredited; the story has in truth not a leg to stand upon except Luke's personal authority as a safe and trustworthy judge of truth and weigher of evidence. Those who first discredit Luke's personal authority, and then attach credibility to his story, are far less reasonable and critical than they who accept the whole.

PART II. Solution of the Problem

Obviously, the truth of the story in Luke 1, 2, can never be demonstrated. There will always remain a large step to be taken on faith. A marvelous event is described in it. They only will accept it who, for other reasons, have come to the conclusion that there is no adequate and rational explanation of the coming of Christianity into the world, except through the direct and "miraculous" intervention of Divine power.

But it is highly important to show that the circumstances with which Luke connects this marvelous event are true, and that, in things which can be tested, he does not fall below the standard of accuracy demanded from the ordinary historians.

Again, those who hold Luke's statement about the enrollment to be a mere blunder ought to give some explanation of the way in which the blunder originated. It is generally stated as an explanation that Luke was dependent on Josephus for the facts of general history which he mentions; and that, as he found in Josephus an account of "the Great Enrollment" made by Quirinius in AD. 6-8, he erroneously connected this enrollment with the birth of Christ.

In discussing this suggested explanation, I shall lay no stress on the steadily growing consensus of opinion that all attempts to prove the dependence of Luke on Josephus have failed, and that Luke's work was composed before Josephus's work on *Jewish Antiquities* was published; for it is possible to maintain that the error was made through confusion and misunderstanding of some other historian›s statement. Luke, who was not born when the events in question occurred, was dependent on some earlier authority or other for his knowledge of the Roman circumstances which he mentions; and the possibility of error arising must be admitted.

But it is necessary to realize clearly how much is involved in the assumption that such an error was made. It is implied not merely that Luke misplaced that important event – fundamental in the Roman organization of Palestine – "the great census"; but also that he distorted the character of that census, which was, beyond all doubt, conducted on the Roman system without the slightest regard to tribal connection, and that he used this distortion of the census to explain why a family belonging to Nazareth came to be present in Bethlehem. Such a series of blunders of a very gross type cannot have been mere slips or mistakes due to ignorance. They bear on their face the character of deliberate invention. They have been concocted for a purpose, *viz.*, to lend verisimilitude to the tale that Jesus was born in Bethlehem. But a tale which is buttressed by such shameful falsifications loses all claim on our belief. And what can we say about a historian who concocts such a series of inventions? What condemnation could be too strong for his shameful conduct? What words too sharp to characterize his imposture?

I put the question to any reasonable person: Is it consistent with human nature that a writer who claims to be earnestly setting forth the simple facts should begin with so impudent a series of fabrications? Can any reasonable judge believe that the author who wrote the rest of the two books could be guilty of such deliberate deception?

Another explanation may perhaps be offered, *viz.*, that Luke did not himself invent the connection between the birth of Jesus and this fraudulent census, but that he incautiously adopted a series of errors which had either grown in popular tradition or been invented by some older writer.

In the first place, we reply, oriental tradition does not take this character: it does not invent such a circumstantial historical setting, whose aim is to work an incident into a place in Roman Imperial history. The census would obviously have been introduced here, not by popular fancy, but by the calculated invention of a person trying to give plausibility to a fiction.

Secondly, Luke's work has all the appearance of being the first attempt to show the place which early Christian history occupied in the general history of the empire: the author is evidently taking the Gospel from his earlier authorities, and on the ground of his own historical inquiries stating its place in Roman history, a subject in which his Jewish authorities took no interest: probably, therefore, he is not dependent on older Christian writers for his statements about the census This is, I think, generally admitted.

PART II. Solution of the Problem

Thirdly, Luke devotes much care to the relations of early Christianity to the Roman state; it was easy for him to acquire correct knowledge as to the Roman census; and, if he allowed a statement on that subject to find a place in his book, he makes himself responsible for it in the fullest sense.

---

[31] Westcott, *Gospel of St. John*, p. 78.
[32] *Ein allgemeiner Reichscensus war dazu weder nöthig noch zweckmässig* are his exact words (Augustus und seine Zeit, Part 1., vol. 2., p. 923).
[33] I do not mean to imply that Mommsen has shown any disposition to accept Luke›s evidence on this point. On the contrary, he dismisses it as a mere mistaken inference from Josephus.
[34] On this see chapter 7.

Chapter 6.
LUKE'S ACCOUNT OF THE ENROLLMENT

LUKE wrote for readers belonging to the civilized Graeco-Roman world; and he conceived the History which he presented to his readers as occupying a place in the general history of the Roman world. He often speaks of "the world"; but to him "the world" was strictly the Roman world, and any order issued by Augustus affected the whole world, as he says in 2:1. Accordingly, at important stages in the action, he inserts a few brief notes, just sufficient to show the position of his subject in the general history of the empire.

The most important of these notes is contained in the following words, 2:1-4, which we give according to the Revised Version:

Now it came to pass in those days, there went out a decree from Caesar Augustus that all the world should be enrolled. This was the first enrollment, made when Quirinius was governing Syria. And all went to enroll themselves, every one to his own city. And Joseph also went up from Galilee, out of the city of Nazareth, into Judea, to the city of David, which is called Bethlehem, because he was of the house and family of David – to enroll himself with Mary his wife.

It might seem hardly necessary to state that in this passage of Luke the term "world," οἰκουμένη, must be understood as the "Roman world, and not the entire earth with all its inhabited lands. But some modern scholars actually charge it as an error that this passage makes an order of Augustus effective throughout the whole earth, whereas the order would have no force except in the Roman empire. Accordingly we must point out that in several places Luke uses the same term "world" when he obviously is speaking only of the Roman empire. To the citizens of the empire all the rest of the earth often passed out of mind; and when they spoke of the world their view was restricted to the Roman world. So, for example, Demetrius, the silversmith of Ephesus, spoke about the

State-Goddess Diana, "whom all Asia and the world worshippeth," *i.e.*, to worship whom the whole province Asia and the Roman empire send their representatives and their crowds of visitors. Again, Paul and Silas were accused before the magistrates of Thessalonica because they had "turned the world upside down"; the accusers were not thinking of the disturbance of order among the outer barbarians, but only in many parts of the Roman empire. Similarly, any ordinary rational interpretation will recognize that Luke 2:1 speaks of the order of Augustus as issued for the whole Roman empire.

What was the extent of "the world" or "the Roman world," of which Luke speaks?

It included, of course, Italy and the organized Roman provinces. But, further, Luke evidently considered that it included the dependent kingdoms, such as Judea, for he describes this order as being carried out in the kingdom of Herod. That such was his point of view seems not to be appreciated by the scholars who ridicule the whole episode; and hence they think that he contradicts himself, when he speaks as if this order extended to the kingdom of Herod.

The question then arises whether it is justifiable to regard these dependent kingdoms, Judea and others, as forming part of the Roman world.

This question Strabo, writing about AD. 19, answers emphatically in the affirmative. In the last chapter of his *Geography* he gives a description of the Roman empire as it was when he was writing about AD. 19. He describes it as extending over the entire coasts of the Mediterranean Sea, and he expressly includes in it the western part of the African coast (Mauretania) which was ruled by King Ptolemy, who had just recently succeeded his father Juba II. Some parts of this empire are, he says, governed by kings, while part is in the form of provinces. There are also subject to the Romans certain dynasts,[35] and chiefs, and priests: and these live according to certain national laws. He distinguishes this whole empire, containing these various territories and governments and provinces, from the non-Roman and barbarian world. He declares that in the part of the empire which is directly under the authority and power of the emperor there are not merely Roman governors of three grades sent from Rome by himself, but also kings, and dynasts, and native officials of lower degree.

Strabo uses several expressions which show how completely he considered these kingdoms to be part of the Roman world. He defines the entire complex of territories as "the possessions of the Romans," τὰ τούτων; he speaks of συμπάσης χώρας τῆς ὑπὸ Ῥωμαίοις; and he describes how the Romans. obtained them, προσεκτήσαντο

Moreover, it is impossible to suppose that Augustus, when he defeated Mark Antony, abandoned the suzerainty which the latter had certainly exercised over many lands, and gave away to independent kings what had once belonged to Rome. The eastern parts of Asia Minor had been treated by Antony as subject to his own absolute authority. When he pleased, he set up a king over part of them; when he chose, he degraded the king. But whoever was the king, Antony claimed from him contributions and military service; and they all sent or led their troops to swell the army of their supreme lord at Actium. It would be irrational to suppose that Augustus, who claimed to be the champion of Rome against Antony, abandoned great territories which Antony had held to be under Rome.

We cannot, therefore, doubt that Strabo expresses the view held by Augustus and by all Rome, that the territory ruled by these dependent kings was part of the Roman empire. They were subject kings, and not free from the suzerainty of Rome.

Appian[36] describes the subject kings whom Antony appointed, including Herod, as paying tribute. We cannot doubt that the same was the case under Augustus. The empire did not abandon its claim to gain something from these kings; and Augustus would not gain less than Antony had gained. On the other hand, it seems to have been left to the discretion of the native rulers to govern and to collect revenue according to native customs and laws. Strabo, in his final chapter; distinguishes between the provinces, to which governors and collectors of taxes were sent from Rome, and the countries subject to Rome, but governed by native princes according to native laws.

Further, Strabo on p. 671 describes the intention of the Romans in setting up these subject kings. He is speaking of Cilicia Tracheia, but he expresses the Roman theory as it was applied generally. Some of the subject countries were specially difficult to govern, either on account of the unruly character of the inhabitants, or because the natural features of the land lent themselves readily to brigandage and piracy. As these countries must be either administered by Roman governors or ruled by kings, it was considered that kings would more efficiently control their restless subjects, being permanently on the spot and having soldiers always at command. But the history of the following century shows how, step by step and district by district, these countries were incorporated in the adjacent Roman provinces, as a certain degree of discipline and civilization was imparted to the population by the kings, who built cities and introduced the Graeco-Roman customs and education.

It appears, therefore, that when Luke counts the kingdom of Herod part of "the Roman World," his point of view agrees with the ideas expressed by Strabo and held generally in the empire.

The decree of Augustus which Luke mentions is commonly interpreted as ordering that a single census should be held of the whole Roman world. This is not a correct interpretation of Luke's words. He uses the present tense (ἀπογράφεσθαι πᾶσαν τὴν οἰκουμένην), and he means that Augustus ordered enrollments to be regularly taken, according to the strict and proper usage of the present tense. What Augustus did was to lay down the principle of systematic "enrollment" in the Roman world, not to arrange for the taking of one single census.

It deserves notice that Malalas, who took the false sense from Luke and describes Augustus as ordering that a single enrollment should be made, unconsciously changes the expression and uses the aorist[37] where Luke uses the present tense. Similarly, when Luke tells that Joseph went up for enrollment on one definite occasion, he uses the aorist (ἀνέβη and ἀπογράψασθαι).

Thereafter the text of Luke proceeds naturally: "This was the first enrollment, while Quirinius was administering Syria; and all persons proceeded to go for enrollment each to his own city". Here the presential tenses (ἀπογράφεσθαι and ἐπορεύοντο) are necessitated by the sense: all persons, individually and severally, repaired to their proper cities for their respective enrollment. In the series of enrollments, which were inaugurated by the orders of Augustus, the first was the one with which the story is concerned; and Joseph, like the rest, went up from Galilee out of the city of Nazareth into Judea, to the city of David, which is called Bethlehem, because he was of the house and family of David.

From this passage, then, it appears that Luke's conception of the procedure in the Roman empire was as follows: Augustus ordered a systematic numbering to be made in the empire. This system of numbering went on for a time, or more probably permanently, and hence the "first" of the series is here defined as the occasion on which the story turns. We may assume unhesitatingly that, if any such system was inaugurated, it would be periodic, recurring regularly either once a year or after a definite term of years.

It is not stated or implied by Luke that the system was actually put into force universally. The principle of universal enrollments for the empire was laid down by Augustus; but universal application of the principle is not mentioned That point was a matter of indifference to Luke. What he implies, indubitably, is that the system was put into force in Syria, for it would be quite irrational that he should speak as he does, unless declare that Luke refers to a hitherto unsuspected fact in the methods of Imperial administration.

But, if our interpretation of Luke's words is correct, we must frankly admit that his credit as a historian is staked on this issue: there was a periodical numbering or enrollment in the Syrian province, and Christ was born actually during the time when the first enrollment of the series was being made in Palestine.

We observe that Luke knew about more than one "enrollment" or census (to use the strict Roman term). In 2:2 he speaks of a certain census as "the first"; in Acts 5:37 he mentions the census," *i.e.*, the great census, meaning the epoch-making census taken about AD. 7, when Judea had just been incorporated in the Roman empire as part of the province of Syria. According to the proper and accepted canons of interpretation in ancient literature, he must be understood in these expressions to distinguish between the first census and the great census. In an ordinary Greek writer the distinction would be unhesitatingly drawn. Why should some scholars assume that Luke thought there had been one single census, as to the date of which he was in a the system had been in force for a time, at least, throughout the Syrian lands. Further, it is not easy to admit that Luke could have used these words, unless the system had come into permanent use.

We conclude, then, that if Luke's authority is trustworthy, there must have prevailed during the first century a system of numbering the population at periodic intervals in the Syrian province, and probably elsewhere in the Eastern lands, or even in the whole empire.

If one had ventured ten years ago to draw this conclusion from the words of Luke, it would have been regarded as a *reductio ad absurdum* of his statement. The idea that such a system could have existed in the East, without leaving any perceptible signs of its existence in recorded history, would have been treated with ridicule as the dream of a fanatical devotee, who could believe anything and invent anything in support of the testimony of Luke. But now such revelations of order and method in the Roman Imperial Government, unmentioned and unheeded by historians, have resulted from epigraphic and archaeological investigation, that it is no longer so hazardous to declare that Luke refers to a hitherto unsuspected fact in the methods of Imperial administration.

But, if our interpretation of Luke's words is correct, we must frankly admit that his credit as a historian is staked on this issue: there was a periodical numbering or enrolment in the Syrian province, and Christ was born actually during the time when the first enrolment of the series was being made in Palestine.

We observe that Luke knew about more than one "enrolment" or *census* (to use the strict Roman term). In 2:2 he speaks of a certain census as " the first" ; in Acts 5:37 he mentions " *the* census,» i.e., the great census, meaning the epoch-making census taken about A.D. 7, when Judæa had just been incorporated in the Roman empire as part of the province of Syria. According to the proper and accepted canons of interpretation in ancient literature, he must be understood in these expressions to distinguish between the first census and the great census. In an ordinary Greek writer the distinction would be unhesitatingly drawn. Why should some scholars assume that Luke thought there had been one single census, as to the date of which he was in a state of utter confusion, when he uses language which in the simple and natural interpretation indicates two different census? A scholar should never start by assuming that the author whom he is interpreting is wrong; but to say that Luke in these two passages refers to one and the same census, is to fasten an error upon him at the outset, by disregarding the distinction indicated in his words.

Clement of Alexandria evidently understood the words of Luke in the same way as we have interpreted them. He speaks of the occasion when first they ordered Enrollments to be made.[38]

It is hardly possible to avoid inferring from these words of Clement that he knew of some system of enrollments, either in the empire as a whole, or at least in the province of Syria. His use of the plural and of the word "first" force this inference upon us.

Further, we shall find in chapter 7 that Clement, as residing in Egypt, was familiar with the Egyptian system of periodic enrollments. He could hardly avoid writing with this system in his mind, and his words imply beyond a doubt that he thought of some system of enrollments in Palestine. I do not see how any fair and unprejudiced critic can fail to conclude that Clement, rightly or wrongly, believed that the same system of periodic enrollments was maintained in Egypt and in Syria.

Again, Clement expressly says that the system of enrollments in Syria began with the one at which the birth of Christ occurred. Luke in all probability was his sole ultimate authority for connecting the birth of Christ with the first enrollment, he, no doubt, saw the statement also in other authorities, but they in their turn probably got it, whether immediately or ultimately, from Luke. But it is not so certain that Clement had no other authority than Luke for his belief that the system began in the reign of Augustus. He knew the system from his own experience in Egypt. It had recurred there regularly throughout his own life, and long before his time. It must have been a matter of common knowledge in his time what was the origin of the system. We are, I think, fully justified in quoting Clement as believing that the system of enrollments which he saw round him in Egypt, and which he thought or knew to be also practiced in Syria, began from Augustus and was made according to the, orders of Augustus.

A suggestion has been made that the Indictional Periods of fifteen years, which formed so important a feature in the administration of the later Roman empire, began to run from the census of Quirinius. On this theory the first census was taken in the year 3 BC. as the beginning of the first Indictional Period. But it can be shown positively that the Indictional System did not prevail under the early empire. The Indictions are an invention of the fourth century; and not merely are those periods unknown in earlier time, but a contradictory system existed.[39] Moreover, it is not easy to bring the evidence as to the duration of Herod›s reign into consistence with the theory that he lived till 3 BC.

Our whole theory is based on the determination of the periodical enrollment system in the early empire; and for this fortunate discovery we are indebted to the wonderful progress of research in Egypt during the last few years.

---

[35] This title was given to certain princes, *e. g.*, those who ruled Ketis in Cilicia Tracheia.

[36] *Bell. Civil.*, 5., 75.

[37] ὥστε ἀπογραφῆναι πᾶσαν τὴν ὑπ' αὐτὸν γενομένην γῆν καὶ ἣν πρώην εἶχον Ῥωμαῖοι, Malalas, p. 226.

[38] ὅτε πρῶτον ἐκέλευσαν ἀπογραφὰς γενέσθαι, Strom., 1., 21, 147.

[39] Mr. Grenfell notes, «it is absolutely certain that the indictions began in A. D. 312, and not before," as is shown by one of the Rainer papyri.

Chapter 7.
ENROLLMENT BY HOUSEHOLDS IN EGYPT

RECENTLY, three different scholars announced about the same time, and independently of one another, the discovery that periodical enrollments were made in Egypt under the Roman empire, and that the period was not of fifteen years, as in the later system of indictions, but of fourteen years. The same Greek term is used in the Egyptian documents and in Luke to indicate the census: they were called "Enrollments," *Apographai*.

Mr. Kenyon of the British Museum had slightly the priority in briefly declaring that these "Enrollments" obeyed a cycle of fourteen years; but Dr. Wilcken followed him within a month or two with an elaborate paper, and shortly afterwards Dr. Viereck with another, discussing their period, nature and purpose.[40] The three papers are the authority for what is here stated on the subject.

The facts relating to the "Enrollments" in Egypt are deduced from the actual census papers, many of which have been found (usually in a more or less fragmentary condition). The census was always taken after the end of the year to which it belongs; thus, for example, a census paper dated in the end of the year AD. 90-91 contains a statement of the facts required for the enrollment of 89-90, and so on. The purpose evidently was to include in each enrollment all children born before the end of the first year of the census period, which we shall henceforth call the periodic year. All dates in these documents are given according to the Egyptian way of reckoning; and the Egyptian year, which began on the twenty-ninth day of August, was at the basis of the whole census system in Egypt. It is proved that enrollments were made for the years ending in the summer of AD. 90, 104, 118, 132 and so on till 230. An enrollment also took place under Vespasian, but its date is not fixed by the evidence. There can, however, be no doubt that Dr. Viereck is right in placing it for the year 75-76.[41]

Though the Egyptian year was employed, the census was carried out by Roman officials, and formed part of the Imperial system of administration.

It was the habit of the Romans in the East to adapt their arrangements to the custom of the country. They did not force the natives to adopt the Roman system of arranging the year and the months, but rather modified their practice to suit the native year, using an Asian year in the Province Asia, an Egyptian year in the Province Egypt, and so on. As the beginning and end of the years varied greatly in different Eastern provinces – all, however, being now solar years, like the Roman – we shall throughout these pages speak of the Roman year; and the reader will understand that in each province it has to be translated into the native year there employed. Censorinus mentions, as was to be expected, that the years of the Imperial system – *anni Augustorum* – were counted from the first of January: they differed in this from the years of any individual emperor›s reign, which during the first century were usually reckoned from the day on which the reign began, though during the second century the habit of reckoning them from the first of January became general.

Accordingly, instead of mentioning the enrollment for the Egyptian year falling in AD. 89-90, we shall call it the enrollment for the Roman year AD. 90. The periodic years, then, are as follows: BC. 23, BC. 9, AD. 6, 20, 34, 48, 62, 76, 90, 104, 118, 132, 146, 160, 174, 188, 202, 216, 230, 244, 258, 272, 286, 300, 314, 328.

In every case, of course, the actual enumeration began after the periodic year was ended, though the enumeration is called in the documents the enrollment of the past (periodic) year. Usually the enrollment paper is dated late in the following year; people were allowed to make their declaration at any time during the following year, and as human nature will have it, most people delayed until the year was approaching its end.

It appears, therefore, that already under Vespasian a system of periodical enrollments was the rule of Roman administration in Egypt. The existing documents establish its existence from AD. 76 to 230; but the failure of documents attesting its previous or subsequent existence affords no evidence that it began under Vespasian or ended under Alexander Severus. The preservation of papyri is so accidental and precarious, that imperfection and *lacunae* are the rule in every department which they touch upon. We must be grateful for the light they throw on any subject, but it would be absurd to reason, because no fragment of papyrus has been found to attest a fact, that therefore the fact did not occur. The argument *a silentio*, always a dangerous one, is especially dangerous where papyrusfragments are concerned.

On this point Mr. Grenfell writes: "I should admit that the argument *a silentio* cannot yet be used as regards the first century after Christ. About the second and third centuries it is, however, worth something, and also, I think, about the Ptolemaic period.» The silence of the papyri about the period before AD. 76 therefore constitutes no argument that the periodic enrollments began in that year.

At the last moment Mr. Grenfell, in a letter dated 12th Sept., 1898, brings to my knowledge, and the courtesy of the discoverer permits me to mention, that Mr. Kenyon has found, and is on the point of publishing in the forthcoming volume of the *Catalogue of British Museum Papyri,* a document[42] which mentions the enrollment for the eighth year of Nero, AD. 61-62. Mr. Kenyon thinks that it implies also still earlier enrollments. This important discovery will be regarded as a strong confirmation of the theory set forth in the following pages, and printed before I heard of the new evidence. The only argument that could be brought forward against the theory lay in the silence of the papyri; and already that silence is broken for part of the period. [Enrollment of AD. 20, see Preface]

The question, then, must be put – at what time and through whose organizing initiative is the Roman series of enrollments likely to have been begun? The answer to that question is not doubtful. We may appeal with confidence to the students of Roman history, and put the question in this way. We find that under Vespasian a system of periodical enrollments formed a fundamental part of the government of Egypt: these enrollments gave a basis on which a statistical account of the population according to households and place of residence at the beginning of each period could be drawn up. Whom should we expect to have introduced the system?

In the first place every one who has studied the history of Roman provincial administration would reply that Augustus was, in all probability, the originator of this Roman system in Egypt. Any important part of Egyptian administration which was in existence under Vespasian is probably as old as the organization of the country by Augustus. It is well known with what peculiar and jealous and minute care: he regarded that country. No Roman of senatorial or equestrian rank was permitten, even to visit it without special leave from the Emperor. It was considered as the granary of Rome; and it was regulated in the most careful way so that its harvests should be reserved for Roman needs, and its resources should be always calculable and certain, as far as care and forethought could make them so.

It is unnecessary to do more than briefly refer to those facts touching the policy and intentions of Augustus which have been skillfully collected and marshaled by a long succession of writers on this subject – his general survey of the whole empire: the *rationes imperii*, «a sort of balance sheet published periodically»: the *libellus* or *breviarium totius imperii*, a compendium of useful statistics about the kingdoms, the provinces, the allies, etc.

These show how carefully and methodically Augustus organized his splendid machinery of government on the basis of accurate, minute and complete knowledge of everything that concerned the subject peoples, and make it probable that the system of periodic enrollments, which alone rendered a complete statistical account of those peoples possible, originated from him, and formed part of his plan of Imperial administration.

In the second place, the system of periodic enrollments is likely to be as old as Augustus, because it probably rested on a pre-Roman foundation. Every year's discoveries strengthen the proof that the organization of Egypt was brought to a very high degree of perfection long before the Romans entered the country, and increase the probability that the germ or even the complete form of almost every detail of administration was found by Augustus already in existence in Egypt, and was merely adapted by him to Roman needs.

Mr. Grenfell notes that the silence of the Ptolemaic papyri about Household-Enrollment – constitutes an argument against its being an institution of the Ptolemaic period; whereas valuation papers of the class (described later in this chapter) are found not infrequently under the Ptolemies. There must, however, have been in that period some kind of numbering (as Wilcken thinks). Papyri are found c. BC. 3000, "a kind of census list of a household," naming the head of the house, resident female relatives, slaves, and young male children.[43] Two *Apographai* of unusual character. occur,[44] resembling the Household-Enrollment papers more than the Valuation papers, and dated BC. 19 and 18, before the Periodic Household-Enrollment system was organized.

The probability remains that Augustus originated a new system in Egypt of Periodic Enrollment-by-Households, developing some previously existing system of numbering the population.

In the third place, as we saw in the preceding chapter, Clement of Alexandria believed that the system of enrollments originated from Augustus; and he expresses the general opinion held in Egypt at the end of the second century.

In the fourth place, chronological reasons suggest that the enrollments come down from the organization of Augustus, because the cycle leads us back to the year BC. 23, from which dates the Imperial rule of Augustus in the most formal and complete sense. The Roman emperors, beginning from Augustus, reckoned the years of their reign according to their tenure of the *tribunicia potestas*, which constituted them "Champions of the Commons"; Augustus received the tribunician power on 27th June, BC. 23; and the number of years in his Imperial title is reckoned invariably in all later inscriptions from that date. The Coincidence that the Enrollment Cycle was arranged according to the official years of Augustus's reign, is conclusive in favor of the view that Augustus inaugurated the system of periodical enrollments.

This coincidence, also, shows with almost complete certainty that the Fourteen-Years'-Cycle was not devised in Egypt, or for Egypt alone. Mr. Grenfell points out to me that in Egypt the reign of Augustus was invariably reckoned from the taking of Alexandria, the first year being considered to begin on 29th August, BC. 30; and there is not a trace of any other reckoning of his reign in the country. Had the Enrollment-Cycle been an Egyptian matter simply, it is in the last degree improbable that it would have been arranged according to the years of the tribunician power.

On the other hand, that was the natural system in general Imperial matters. It was the only method of reckoning which was known universally throughout the empire: it was employed in every official statement of the Emperor's title: it was sometimes used even in dating private inscriptions.[45]

The use of this epoch, further, proves in all probability that the Enrollment was, as Luke says, actually held first for the year BC. 9. It could not be devised until after the reign began, for the epoch was unknown until the epoch-making event had occurred; and, after it had occurred, no time remained to arrange all the details for an Imperial enrollment for the current year. Hence we find a different style of enrollment paper used in Egypt in the years BC. 19 and 18.

We see also why the Egyptian year 24-23, and not 23-22, was taken as that correspondent to the Roman year 23. Augustus's reign began during the Egyptian year 24-23, two months before the end of that year on 29th August. Thus the reign of Augustus began officially in the Egyptian year BC. 24-23. On the other hand, in any country where the year began in the spring, the official year 1 of Augustus would be the year BC. 23-22; and the year 15, which was the first periodic year, would be BC. 9-8.

These reasons justify the reasonable confidence that Augustus arranged a system of periodical "enrollments" in Egypt. As the system is fixed according to the year BC. 23, in which the fully formed constitutional Principate was organized and the reign of Augustus in the official reckoning began, the arrangement of this system must have taken place later than that year. The system of enrollments must therefore be distinguished from the operation called by Marquardt[46] the provincial census, which began to be taken in Gaul in BC. 27.

The latter operation was intended to form the basis on which the taxation of the provinces of the empire should be regulated. It was repeated from time to time throughout the period of the empire, and was an essential part of the orderly working of the Imperial administration. That taxation should be proportionate to wealth was a Roman principle, and without frequent revaluation of property it was impossible to secure a fair apportionment of taxation. Augustus fully recognized the vast importance of making correct valuation of property in the provinces, as securing both fair taxation and a more lucrative revenue for the State.

Such enumeration and valuation of property was confined, as a rule, to Roman provinces, and was often made as soon as any new province was incorporated in the empire. Such, for example, was the case in Palestine when Quirinius, in his second Syrian governorship, made that country part of the empire. The novel proceedings on that occasion, and the strict inquisition into value of property, brought vividly home to the Jews that they were now wholly reduced to servitude under a foreign power, and led to much disorder and rebellion. The name census was used by the Romans to denote this characteristic institution. In modern usage the term census denotes the periodic numbering of the people, without valuation of property. In this study we use the terms "valuation" or "rating" and "enrollment".

But the system of periodic enrollments in Egypt is quite different from the system of rating and valuation. The latter system also existed in Egypt; many census papers are preserved among the papyri, and Wilcken gives several examples of them on pp. 231-240 of the article which we have quoted above. These valuations seem to have been made annually;[47] and it is often stated in the papers that the census is taken according to the orders of the governor of the province. They contain an enumeration and precise definition of all property in land, houses, and live stock[48] belonging to the enumerator, often also a statement whether the property is free from debt or mortgage, and often an estimate of the money value, of the whole. Where there is no estimate of value, it is understood that the value is unchanged from previous valuations and can be found in the older official registers.

The same verb ἀπογράφομαι is used in both kinds of papyri, and both operations seem to have been termed *Apographai*. But the periodic enrollment papers are distinguished by other criteria besides the want of statistics about property and money value; they are dated according to the year of the reigning emperor, and contain no reference to the orders of the governor; they state accurately and exactly which periodic enrollment they are intended for; and they always use the phrase "Enrollment-by-Household", ἀπογραφὴ κατ' οἰκίαν. These periodic enrollments according to the Four-teen-Years›-Cycle[49] were therefore closely connected with the existing households, and served as basis for an enumeration of the total population. This operation obviously corresponds much more closely than the other kind of Egyptian census to the «enrollment» alluded to by Luke; and we shall therefore always allude to it as the enrollment system, or, more accurately, enrollment-by-household.

The enrollment papers were filled up and sent in to the proper official by the heads of households. In the enrollment paper, the householder specified the house, or part of a house, which belonged to him; he declared that he was formally enrolling himself and his family for the house-to-house enrollment of the past year, twenty-eight of the Emperor Commodus, or whatever else the case was. But, if the owner did not live in the house himself, he enrolled only the tenants; if he kept lodgers, he enrolled himself, his family and the lodgers. He gave a complete enumeration of all the individuals who lived in the house, children, relatives, etc. In one case, twenty-seven persons are enumerated in one paper by a householder. No statement of income or of the money value of the house is given in the enrollment papers.

Thus, according to our theory, the nature of the case led the Romans to adopt a double system, which presents a remarkable analogy to our modern methods. We have an enumeration of the people every ten years, the census: the Romans numbered the people every fourteen years. We have an annual making up of the valuation roll, and an annual system of income tax returns. The Romans, likewise, found it expedient to require annual valuation of property; but they did not require any estimate of annual income, for they, like the United States, arranged their taxes, not according to income, but according to property.

The intention of this system of enrollment by households has been investigated by Wilcken. It furnished a complete enumeration of the population of Egypt; both provincials and resident Romans had to fill up their enrollment papers and send them in to the proper official. The papers not merely furnished the total numbers of the population; they were also useful in allotting the various burdens of public service, and especially they facilitated the conscription; and finally they gave information which aided in levying the poll-tax, determining the classes of persons who were free from the tax, and the date at which each male became of age to pay it (fourteen), or reached the age of exemption (sixty).[50]

According to Marquardt, 2., p. 199, a poll-tax was levied by the Romans only in countries where it had been customary from ancient times, or where there was for the time no survey of property available to furnish a standard for a more rational kind of tax. He is disposed to consider the *tributum capitis* in the province of Syria as not a poll-tax, but a tax on those engaged in an industrial occupation; but Wilcken seems clearly right in regarding the Syrian tax as a poll-tax, exactly similar to the Egyptian poll-tax.

Thus the Egyptian documents, and the inferences founded on them by comparison with other evidence, have revealed two most important and hitherto unsuspected facts.

(1) In some parts at least of the empire the enrollment and numbering of the population according to their households was a distinct and separate process from the census and valuation, which previously was considered to be the only properly Roman kind of census.

(2) The enrollment by households took place periodically, according to a cycle arranged according to the years of the reign of Augustus in Imperial, but not in Egyptian, reckoning. Probably this system was introduced later than 18 BC.

PART II. Solution of the Problem

NOTE

Papyrus Br. Mus. CCLX. is a poll-tax register of AD. 72-3, based on the Household-Enrollment of 61-2; and references to older poll-tax registers are made, which imply previous Enrollments. In fact the register is part of an existing system of some standing. [The Household-Enrollment of AD. 20 has just been discovered: see Preface].

---

[40] Kenyon in *Classical Review*, March 1893, p. 110; Wilcken in Hermes, 1893, p. 203 ff.; Viereck in *Philologus*, 1893, p. 219 ff. There is a short supplementary paper by Wilcken in *Philologus*, 1893, p. 563.
[41] Confirmed by Mr. Kenyon›s new discovery.
[42] CCLX. 78, 79, and CCLXI. 31, 32.
[43] F. Ll. Griffith, *Law Quart. Rev.*, 1898, p. 44 f.
[44] Grenfell, *An Alex. Erotic Papyrus, etc.,* Nos. 45 and 46.
[45] See *e.g. Varia* 2. in *Classical Review*, Oct., 1898.
[46] *Röm. Staatsrecht*, 2., p. 212 f.
[47] Mr. Grenfell notes, «‹for seem to have been› you might say ‹were›: there are hundreds of instances to show it».
[48] Mr. Kenyon notes, «‹returns of live stock are separate".
[49] The Romans, who counted both initial and final years in each period, would have called it a ‹Fifteen-Years›-Cycle; it was held in years 1, 15, 29, etc. We call that a Cycle of fourteen years.
[50] So Kenyon writes correcting Wilcken›s published statement. In Syria women, as well as men, paid; and the age was fourteen for men, twelve for women, until sixty-five, Ulpian, *Dig.*, L. 15, 3.

Chapter 8.
THE SYRIAN ENROLLMENT IN 8 BC

IN the preceding chapter we have seen that, in all probability, Augustus inaugurated a series of enrollments in Egypt. Now, according to Luke, Augustus laid down the principle that "enrollments" should be made over the whole Roman world; and this assertion stands on a very different level of probability from that which it occupied before the Egyptian discovery. If Luke be wrong, his error has been to extend over the whole Roman world a practice which Augustus established in Egypt. Every one must see that such an extension is not likely to have been made without some justification by the author of Acts, whoever he was. If there is anything certain about him it is that he had neither connection with Egypt nor interest in it, and that he was entirely uninfluenced by Alexandrian thought or Egyptian ideas; he even omits from his Gospel the incident of the flight into Egypt, which a writer connected with Egypt would be most unlikely to do. Such an author is not likely to have known about institutions peculiar to Egypt; and, if he thinks that the system of periodical enrollments, which existed in Egypt, was also found in other parts of the Roman world, there is a strong presumption that such was the case at least in those parts of the world which were best known to him. The reasons stated above, chapters 6 and 7, confirm this presumption.

Other considerations, also, prove that some attempt was made in Syria, whether systematically or sporadically, to number the population Such enumerations can be traced back to the reign of Augustus and to the government of Syria by Quirinius.

An inscription, which was long the subject of keen controversy and was condemned by Mommsen and many others as a forgery,[51] was recently found to be genuine, when half of the long-lost stone on which it was engraved was rediscovered in Venice. In that inscription, which records the career of Q Aemilius Secundus, a Roman officer, who served under Quirinius when governor of Syria, it is mentioned that by the orders of Quirinius he made the «census» of the population of Apameia, enumerating 117,000 citizens. The emphasis laid on the number suggests (though it does not demonstrate) that the numbering of the total population was the chief object of the Apamean «census»; in that case it would correspond to the periodic enrollment by households in Egypt rather than to the annual valuation.

The inscription leaves it uncertain whether the Apamean numbering occurred in the first or second administration of Syria by Quirinius. He is called *legatus Caesaris Syriae*, without *iterum*, but there was no need for expressing in the inscription that he had held the government of Syria on two separate occasions. Our opponents, who hold that there was only one census under Quirinius, are justified in maintaining that this inscription refers to a numbering of the population of Syria, made by Quirinius in AD. 7 concurrently with his census and valuation in Palestine. We, on our side, are, for a different reason, bound to maintain that Quirinius ordered this enrollment of Apameia (and of all the other states of Syria) to be made in AD. 7, as will appear in chapters 9 and 11.

Again, Suidas mentions that Augustus numbered the population of the territory that belonged to the Romans, and it was found to be 4,101,017 men (ἄνδρες). It is obvious that Suidas did not simply invent this number, but had access to some other authority besides Luke (whom he quotes in one of the two places[52] where he refers to this enumeration of the Roman world). The question is how far any confidence can be placed in that other authority. Had he real knowledge at his command?

The number seems so small as to be absurd. Josephus[53] gives the population of Egypt, Alexandria excepted, as 7,500,000. Adding 500,00 as the population of Alexandria, we have the total Egyptian population, 8,000,000. But, according to Suidas, the population of the entire Roman world would not be much more than 21,000,000. Probably the populous countries of Syria and Asia Minor alone contained more than 21,000,000 inhabitants, though we must remember that no slaves were counted in the enrollments.

The most probable supposition is that Suidas is giving an inaccurate account of the total of Roman citizens. A numbering of Roman citizens was three times made by Augustus – 28 BC., 8 BC. and 14 AD. – and the total was in each case between 4,000,000 and 5,000,000. The liability of numbers to corruption is exemplified in the result of Augustus's first 80 census. The Latin text of the *Monumentum Ancyranum*, expressed in Augustus's own words, gives the total as 4,063,000, but the Greek translation gives 4,603,000, while Eusebius has it as 4,164,000. In the third census, Eusebius probably gave the correct total; but Jerome in his Latin version and the Armenian translator have both gone wrong in rendering Eusebius's words. Suidas, finding this total in Eusebius, took it as representing the total population of the empire, instead of the sum of *cives Romant*, an error which was easily made after the time of Caracalla, when all free citizens of the empire were *cives Romani*. Further, like Jerome, he misunderstood the numbers in Eusebius. Syncellus gives the total in still another form.

Thus Suidas, when we trace him back, is found to have been using a distinct and good authority, but to be misunderstanding and misrepresenting it. He throws no light on Luke's statement.

Further, there is a certain amount of positive evidence that "Enrollments" according to the Fourteen-Years'-Cycle were made in Syria and elsewhere. According to Luke, the first enrollment was made a few years BC. in the unknown year of Christ's birth, which is variously fixed, and must have been somewhere between 8 and 3 BC.. On the system that obtained in Egypt, the year 9 BC. would be the beginning of the second period; and the scanty evidence that exists about the general survey of the empire, shows that any enrollment according to the Cycle is not likely to have been made until the beginning of the second period. We find, then, that the year 8 BC. was the one in which the first "enrollment" would naturally begin to be made, if a Cycle was observed; for this enrollment was intended, as has been stated already, to include all children born in 9 BC. Now Tertullian declares that an "enrollment" was made by Sentius Saturninus, who was governor of Syria from about 9 to 7 BC. It is obvious that Tertullian did not make this assertion on Luke's authority, nor with the intention of bolstering up Luke. On the contrary, it has always been a serious problem how his statement can be reconciled with Luke's

PART II. Solution of the Problem

words. It can hardly be doubted that Tertullian was aware of the discrepancy between his own words and those of Luke; but he remains true to his own principle that "this world's things must be tested by its own documents".[54] He had the authority of Roman documents that Sentius Saturninus was the governor in question; and he prefers to follow «this world›s documents». The discrepancy with Luke would not trouble him; his belief was too robust-to be affected by trifles of that kind; but whether or not he understood how the apparent discrepancy arose, he at any rate followed his Roman authority in this detail.

Tertullian's procedure was probably this: he knew that an enrollment period fell in 9 BC. which was the first enrollment; and Roman authorities, either official documents or historians, showed him that Sentius Saturninus was governor of Syria at that time. The only other alternative seems to be that he investigated Roman documents, and found evidence that a census of Syria had been held by Saturninus. In the former case he was aware of the Fourteen-Years'-Cycle; in the latter case he knew of a census of Syria about 9-7 BC. and in either case he is an important yet independent witness in favor of Luke, so far as concerns the reality of a Syrian enrollment about 9-7 BC.

We must observe that it was possible for any one living in the first or second or third century to discover for himself the facts about any of these early enrollments, if he were willing to take a little trouble and show a little care. Accurate observation, registration and preservation of all facts formed the basis of Roman Imperial administration. We know from Pliny[55] that the facts obtained at every census were so carefully preserved that in 48 AD. Claudius could verify from the records of earlier numberings the statement, which a citizen of a small Italian town made about his age; and there can be no doubt that similar careful preservation was the rule everywhere, as is proved in Egypt. Abundant material existed on which, the historian who was willing to take trouble could base an accurate narrative of facts. With an author of ordinary ability and care, serious error could hardly arise except from intention to mislead; though, of course, a slip in some unimportant detail may be made by any man, however careful, and probably none are free from them, not even Mommsen himself, whose grasp of detail is so marvelous.

The discrepancy between Tertullian, who seems to connect the birth of Christ with the enrollment of Saturninus, and Luke, who connects that event with the enrollment of Quirinius, will engage our attention in chapter 11. For the moment our purpose is to show that the Egyptian enrollment periods were observed in Syria and elsewhere. But the existence of such a discrepancy is the conclusive proof that Tertullian had good evidence to trust to. He would never have contradicted Luke as regards the name, unless he had obtained the fact on undeniable authority.

In the same year 8 BC.., in which "enrollments" seem to have been made in Syria and in Egypt, Augustus, as he mentions in his official review of his own life, made a census and found that the total number of Roman citizens in the whole empire was 4,233,000. A similar numbering of Roman citizens had been made by him in 28 BC.

The fact that Augustus's first two enumerations show an interval of twenty years forms no argument against our theory of a Fourteen-Years' Cycle. The first enumeration was made before the plan was initiated, and the second, the initiation of the plan, was fixed according to the epoch of 23 BC.

At any rate, 8 BC. was a marked year in the administration of the city of Rome. In that year, Augustus gave Rome a new municipal organization, dividing it into regions and quarters; and in a certain class of Roman city inscriptions, it is reckoned as the year 1 of an epoch which remained in use for a time. It was not an Imperial epoch; it was merely used in dating some documents connected with the new Roman municipal system, and the year I did not agree with the first of the Fourteen-Years'-Cycle, but was taken at, the: first year in which the new municipal system was actually in existence.

The next periodic year was 6 AD. and the enrollment would, therefore, naturally be taken in the following year, 7 AD. Quirinius was governor of Syria for the second time in 6 and the following years; and he held "the great census" and valuation of Palestine, as Josephus records. Judea was now incorporated in the empire, administered by a *Procurator*, and

PART II. Solution of the Problem

connected with the Province Syria; and a complete set of statistics of the new territory was required as the basis of the Roman organization. "The great enrollment" might, it is true, be plausibly explained as due merely to the necessities of administration in a newly incorporated part of the empire. But it is, at least, an interesting coincidence that it should tally with the beginning of a new Cycle. Moreover, it is practically almost certain that Quirinius made a numbering of the population of Syria in 7 AD. as we have gathered from the inscription of Aemilius Secundus, previously qouted. The natural inference from the known facts is that two operations, one corresponding to the Egyptian periodic enrollment and one corresponding to the Egyptian annual census and valuation, occurred in Palestine in 7 AD.; and that the periodic enrollment at least, if not the other also, was made throughout the province of Syria.

The Cycle beginning 6 AD. seems not to have been observed by Augustus himself in Rome. It is well known that, as he grew old and feeble, his administration became more lax. Possibly, as Luke declares, he intended in 9 BC. to begin a series of "enrollments" for the empire; but, if he had that intention, the idea was too great for the time and was not fully carried into effect. The administrative machinery of the empire was not as yet sufficiently perfect and smooth-working to be able to carry into regular execution such a great idea; and Augustus postponed the next numbering of Roman citizens, until Tiberius was associated with him in the government, when 4,937,000 Roman citizens were numbered, 14 AD. Dion Cassius indeed mentions that in 4 AD. Augustus made a partial census; but that would be two years too early; and, as Mommsen and others have shown, Dion Cassius's account of the various numberings made by Augustus is wrong in almost every case, and his assertion about a census in 4 AD. cannot be credited on his sole authority. Mommsen, therefore, rejects it as an error of Dion's.[56]

The next periodic year fell in 20 AD.; but no evidence survives to show that it was observed in any part of the Roman empire. Perhaps after the numbering of Roman citizens in 14, it was considered unnecessary by Tiberius to hold another in 20; and our authorities hardly ever mention any numberings except of cives Romani.

The following census period began with 34 AD.; and it would appear that the numbering was held in the Province Syria in 35, as was usual. This we gather indirectly from the fact that an attempt was made by King Archelaos to enforce a census after the Roman style in his kingdom of Cilicia Tracheia. Now this kingdom was always considered as a dependency of the Province Syria;[57] and, when any Roman interference in its affairs was needed, the Syrian governor marched an army into the Tracheiotis. Archelaos›s attempt, therefore, implies that the census of Syria was taken in 35, and was observed also in the dependent kingdom of Tracheiotis. It may be regarded as obviously true that Archelaos acted under Roman orders, for the imposition of a Roman custom on the free Cilicians, as if they had been inhabitants of a Roman province, was a curtailment of his rights, which he was not likely to initiate of his own accord, and which a monarch would not allow except under compulsion. But nations which were not thoroughly Romanised strongly objected to the census as a mark of subjection to the foreigner and as a serious step forward in the process of Romanising their country. King Archelaos was considered by his subjects to be weakly helping to impose on them the Roman yoke with his own hand. Disturbances broke out among the Kietai,[58] the leading people of Cilicia Tracheia; and, after the power of King Archelaos had proved insufficient to quell their, rebellion, the presence of Roman troops was required; and finally, in 36 AD. Vitellius, the governor of Syria, sent an army to his aid.

As in "the great enrollment" of Palestine in 7 AD., there was made in Cilicia in 35 AD. both a numbering of the population and a valuation of their property. A simple numbering of the people might not be felt so grievous, but a valuation of property seemed to be the beginning of incorporation in a province.

Some scholars understand that the census among the Kietai was held because they had been subjected to the Roman authority and incorporated in the province. But Tacitus distinctly states that they were subject to Archelaos, and continued to hold out against his troops. His language is quite explicit, and could be misinterpreted only through prejudice. Moreover, if the Kietai had been incorporated in the prov-

PART II. Solution of the Problem

ince, that would show even more conclusively that an enrollment of the province was made in 34-5 AD.

The next periodic year fell in 48; and Tacitus mentions that the Emperor Claudius held a census of the Roman citizens in that year, and numbered 6,944,000. He was personally engaged as censor in the operations at Ostia in the middle of October, 48 AD. The individual householders recorded their age in these numberings, just as they did in the Egyptian enrollments, for Pliny mentions that a citizen of Bononia stated his age as 150; Claudius thereupon ordered that his record in previous census should be examined, and his statements were found to be consistent.[59] This fact, mentioned incidentally by Pliny, proves that several census had previously been taken, and suggests that there was a system and a definite plan in the enumerations. No one who considers the method of the Romans and the orderly character of all their work, will regard it as probable that the taking of these general numberings was left purely to the caprice of the emperor. Some plan and order must have been aimed at, though the weakness or caprice of the emperors might occasionally disturb the order. The existence of some underlying plan is inexorably demanded; and if the plan which existed in Egypt was not common to the whole empire, one asks what was the plan elsewhere, and why the empire followed separate plans in different regions.

Claudius evidently made his numbering a few months too early, before the periodic year was ended.

The succeeding census period, beginning in 62 AD. is not known to have been observed in any part of the Roman world except Egypt (where Mr. Kenyon's new discovery has revealed it); and the Subsequent one, 76 AD. was anticipated in Italy by two years, for Vespasian and Titus held the censorship in 73 and 74, [60] and made all enumeration of Roman citizens.

These facts, most of them only slight in themselves, establish in conjunction a strong case that the periods of the Egyptian enrollments were frequently coincident with the holding of census in some other parts of the empire; and thus the presumption is strengthened that the Egyptian Fourteen-Years'-Cycle has its root in a principle of wider application. This brings us very near to Luke's statement that Augustus laid down a general principle of taking census of the whole Roman world. The supposition that his statement is true has now ceased to be out of keeping with extra-scriptural evidence. On the contrary, Luke's statement supplies the missing principle which holds together and explains and makes consistent all the rest of the evidence. When Luke's evidence is held correct, the other recorded facts fall into line with it, and are seen to be the working of one general principle. Though weakness sometimes failed to carry out the principle, and though in other cases the time was anticipated a little, yet the recorded facts show a clear tendency to conform to the Cycle.

In a number of cases nothing except the census of Roman citizens is recorded. Almost all Romans, with characteristic Roman pride, regarded a census of the subject population as beneath the dignity of historical record. Augustus himself, in that famous record of his achievements, which is commonly known as the *Monumentum Ancyranum*, mentions only his census of Roman citizens. Distinct evidence exists that the first and second periodic enrollments were carried out in Syria; but the Emperor thought them unworthy of notice in his review of his services to the State. Similarly it is only by indirect inference, through the accident that a rebellion was provoked, that we learn of the fourth enrollment in Syria. The Romans of that period did not agree with our estimate of what was most important in their history; and we must be very chary of drawing negative inferences merely from their silence. Evidence about the details of the Augustan system of provincial administration had almost completely perished, until inscriptions began to reveal a few isolated facts.

Hence the silence of Augustus about the scheme of an Imperial census affords no argument against his having projected such a scheme. In his review of his career, Augustus says nothing about the reorganization of the. provincial administration (which, to our judgment, is almost the most important fact in his career); he mentions nothing about the provinces except the colonies which he founded in Pisidia, Gallia, etc., and the colonies are mentioned simply because they were settlements of Roman citizens. He therefore could not, ill accordance with his own plan,

PART II. Solution of the Problem

mention the scheme of numbering the subject population; he only speaks of the numbering of the Romans. Moreover, the principle of periodic enrollments appears not to have been, perhaps, carried out completely, and could not claim a place in the list of the emperor's achievements.

The most important fact is that we have clear evidence, quite independent of Luke, that the first, second and fourth periodic enrollments were observed ill the Province Syria. The evidence for the first is Christian, and is therefore commonly set aside, except when the "critical" – or rather uncritical – theologian desires to bring out that these Christians don't even agree with one another: then he quotes Tertullian.

The evidence for the second. periodic enrollment in Syria lies in the chance preservation of an inscription, ill which a Roman officer recorded his service at Apameia; but this evidence was long discredited as a forgery, made in modern times by some person who wanted' to illustrate Luke, and pretended to have copied the inscription from a stone. The demolition of a house in Venice revealed the stone, and justified the inscription.

The evidence for the fourth periodic inscription is, found in Tacitus. Had the authority been a mere Christian, his words would have been ridiculed and disregarded.

But three occurrences are sufficient to show what was the law of recurrence. If the other evidence is enough to suggest that some system was recognized in Syria, then the three dates show that the Fourteen-Years'-Cycle was the system which was followed there.

Further, we observe that in all three cases it is only by a mere accident that we learn about the occurrence of a census – a casual reference in Terullian's disputation against a heretic: the chance preservation of an inscription in Venice: the fact that a disturbance in a dependent kingdom was too serious for the king's strength, and required the intervention of the Roman arms, and thus rose to the level of dignity required for mention in Tacitus's *Annals*. The ordinary class of inscriptions on stone does not mention events of this kind, except through an occasional chance, as, *e.g.*, that some private: individual was specially concerned with the taking of a census (like Aeimilius Secundus). But we cannot expect many such chances, as have preserved the memory of the three enrollments in Syria.

In Syria there existed the same reasons which are considered by Wilcken to have required the periodic enrollment by households in Egypt. In both countries there existed a poll-tax (which was not a general Roman institution): conscription and imposition of various burdens in the State service were common to all parts of the empire: hence the periodic enrollments would enable the machinery of government to work with much greater ease and certainty in Syria.

Any rational and scholarly criticism must accept the conclusion: There was a system of periodic enrollment in the Province Syria, according to a Fourteen-Years'-Cycle (in the modern expression – Fifteen-Years'-Cycle in the Roman form), and the first enrollment was made in the year 8 BC. (strictly the Syrian year beginning in the spring of 8 BC.).

The fact that there exists no evidence of such frequent taking of census in Syria, as we suppose, constitutes no disproof of our theory. The evidence has perished. Twenty years ago no one dreamed to what a degree of minuteness and perfection the registration of inhabitants, property and values in Egypt was carried by the Romans. The evidence seemed to have perished. Now the graves and rubbish-heaps of Egypt have begun to give up their evidence; and our knowledge of Roman provincial administration has entered on a new stage. But elsewhere we cannot hope for such discoveries as in Egypt, for other climates are too moist to allow paper to survive. But the analogy of Egyptian administration is a strong argument as regards Syria; and, if Augustus instituted periodic enrollments in Egypt, the evidence of Luke, implying that he ordered a similar system in the whole empire, and that the system was carried into effect in Syria, has every probability in its favor and will be accepted by every candid historian.

We have the evidence of Justin Martyr[61] a native of Syria, writing about 150 AD., that the tabulated information gathered from the periodic enrollments of the province was preserved, and might be consulted by

PART II. Solution of the Problem

any who doubted the evidence of Luke. Writing to the emperor, the Caesars, the senate, and the people of Rome, he tells them that they can learn the facts regarding the birth of Christ from the registers made under Quirinius. It is obvious that Justin had not himself consulted the registers. He merely knew that they existed and might be consulted. The facts he takes from Luke, and challenges all to disprove them by appeal to the registers.

Similarly Tertullian[62] appeals to the letter of Marcus Aurelius, in which he had informed the senate of the important service rendered by Christian soldiers in the German war. He had not seen the letter himself, but he knew that all such documents addressed to the senate were preserved, and challenged his readers to consult the letter for themselves.

It would be quite fair to quote Tertullian as evidence (if any evidence were needed) that such Imperial letters were preserved in official records; and similarly it is quite fair to quote Justin as evidence that the registers of the Syrian enrollments were preserved and might be consulted by those who wished.

Mr. Kenyon writes that natives of Egypt refer to previous enrollments as evidence of relationship, etc. Josephus, *Vit.*, 1., apparently is quoting similar enrollment-registers, when he speaks of the evidence for his family history.

Justin himself had no desire or need to consult the registers in order to be convinced. It was quite enough for him that Luke recorded the facts; and he asked no further evidence. As to questions of date and officials he felt no interest. Perhaps he may have interpreted Luke's words as referring to Quirinius's second government of Syria in 6-7 AD.; but he styles him procurator of Palestine, which does not suit that or any office held by him, for the procuratorship was an equestrian position, while Quirinius was of senatorial rank. But it tended to convince the Romans that the Gospels as a whole were true, if these little details were found to be correctly stated; and therefore he challenges his readers to verify them for themselves.

[51] Absolutely the only reason for thinking it to be a forgery was that it mentioned the census of Quirinius, and therefore seemed to give some support to Luke. But as this might be the historical census of Quirinius in AD. 7, the support was very slight and indirect; and, if a forger were inventing a support for Luke, he would hardly be content with such a small result for his work. See Mommsen in *Ephemeris Epigraphica*, 4., p. 588, on the rediscovery of the stone.

[52] Suidas, *s. vv.* Ἀπογραφὴ and Αὐγοῦστος.

[53] Bell. *Jud.*, 2., 16, 4.

[54] *De uis enim instrumentis saecularia probari necesse est* (*de Cor.* 7).

[55] *Nat. Hist.*, 7., 48 (159).

[56] Mommsen, *Monum. Ancyran.*, ed. 2., p. 37.

[57] Strictly the province was termed *Syria et Cilicia et Phoenice*.

[58] Tacitus, *Annals*, 6., 41, and Wilhelm, *Arch. Epigr. Mittheilungen*, 1894, p. 1 ff.

[59] Tacitus, *Annals*, 9., 25, 31; Suetonius, *Claud.*, 16; Pliny, *Nat. Hist.*, 7., 48 (159).

[60] Beginning April 73 (according to Chambalu, *de magistrat. Flaviorum*, quoted by Goyau, *Chronologie de l'Emp. Rom., s. a.*) their office lasted eighteen months. See Pliny, *Nat. Hist.*, 7., 49 (162).

[61] *Apolog.*, 1., 34. Felix, governor of Egypt, is mentioned in it, and he governed Egypt about 150.

[62] *Apolog.* 5.

PART II. Solution of the Problem

Chapter 9.
KING HEROD'S ENROLLMENT

THE first enrollment in Syria was made in the year 8-7 BC., but a consideration of the situation in Syria and Palestine about that time will show that the enrollment in Herod's kingdom was probably delayed for some time later.

Herod occupied a delicate and difficult position on the throne of Judea. On the one hand he had to comply with what was required of him by the Imperial policy; he was governing for the Romans a part of the empire, and he was bound to spread western customs and language and civilization among his subjects, and fit them for their position in the Roman world. Above all, the prime requirement was that he must maintain peace and order; the Romans knew well that no civilizing process could go on, so long as disorder and disturbance and insecurity existed in the country. Herod's duty was to keep the peace and naturalize the Graeco-Roman civilization in Palestine.

On the other hand, he must soothe the feelings and accommodate himself to the prejudices of the jealous and suspicious people whom he governed. He could not hope to keep the peace among them, unless he humored their prejudices. They hated and despised Roman ideas, and they were intensely attached to their own customs. Their customs had all a religious foundation, and they could not comply with foreign requirements without doing violence to their deep-rooted pride of religion and their lofty contempt for the pagans by whom they were surrounded. Everything Roman was to them a heathen abomination; and, if Herod seemed to them to be forcing on them anything Roman, insurrection was almost certain to follow. But it was absolutely necessary to prevent insurrection, which was likely to make Augustus quite as angry with him as with the insurgents.

On the whole, Herod had been successful in his ambiguous position. He built many fortresses and many cities of the Graeco-Roman type, with temples of the Graeco-Roman gods, beginning with the god incarnate, the emperor himself, whose refusal to accept Divine honors was not very much regarded in the eastern lands. That was the approved method of spreading the Graeco-Roman civilization. The "city" was originally a Greek creation, and every city tended towards the cosmopolitan type of the Roman empire. Education, luxury, commerce, imitation of western manners, dislike for the national and "barbarian" manners, use of the Greek language, were encouraged in the crowded and feverish line of cities; and the national piety and the national exclusiveness found it more difficult to maintain themselves in their old strength.

But Jerusalem was left still Hebrew in spite of the theater and amphitheater and fortress called Antonia, which Herod built. There was really a double life in the ancient city, and Herod put on the appearance of fostering both. If he adorned the city with splendid buildings after the Greek fashion, he also was careful to rebuild the Jewish Temple with far greater magnificence than of old. He would show himself a true king of the Jews. He pretended to conform to the Jewish Law, and did so in some matters of form and ceremony. He refused to permit his sister Salome's marriage with the Arabian Syllaeus, unless the latter conformed to the Jewish law.

Herod never entered the holy place, as Pompey did. He allowed the religious ritual free play. He never attempted to prevent any of the priestly ceremonial. He never assumed to himself ally of the priestly functions. When the temple was being built, only the priests were used in constructing the sanctuary, so that the holy place might never be profaned by any other than a priest's foot or hand. He avoided heathen emblems and devices on his coins and on the buildings of Jerusalem. He: permitted the Sanhedrin to continue during his reign, and to exercise a shadow of its ancient power doubtless only in religious matters, and subject, doubtless, to constraint from the ever-present thought of what would be the result to themselves, if they did anything that Herod disliked.

Thus Herod kept up the appearance of maintaining national feeling, of defending the Jewish cause against all foreigners, and of respecting national ideas and prejudices. He governed his action on the natural and obvious principle. He did not attempt to force the Jews to do anything that was distinctly non-national and non-Jewish; he maintained their religious ceremonial, and refrained from obtruding on them personally anything that was offensive to them. The theaters and other pagan abominations were for the accursed heathen; but the Jews could do as they pleased about such unholy things. They tolerated Herod, and he did not outrage them.[63]

But, in spite of all his care to comply with the Roman requirements, towards the end of his life Herod fell into disgrace with Augustus. He had made war on the Arabians; and Syllaeus, the Arabian minister, who was in Rome, obtained the ear and the confidence of Augustus, and persuaded him that Herod had made war on his own authority without Roman permission. Augustus was very angry, and wrote to Herod that, whereas hitherto he had treated the Jewish king as a friend, he would henceforth treat him as a subject.[64]

The time when this letter was written is, uncertain. Schuerer is inclined to date it in 8 BC., probably rightly. Lewin, *Fasti Sacri*, p. 109, places it in 7 BC.

These emphatic words, coming from an emperor whose words were always well weighed and weighty, soon bore fruit in action, as we may be certain. Nothing is related by Josephus as to the exact form that the Roman action took; but he tells very emphatically how much Herod was embarrassed by the loss of Augustus's favor. In one point, Luke comes to our aid. He shows that Herod was ordered to consider that the recent orders for an enrollment in the Province Syria applied also to his kingdom and must be obeyed.

A probable conjecture places at this point the oath of fidelity to the Emperor, which the whole Jewish people was ordered to take, and which 6000 Pharisees refused. It is natural that, when the king was degraded to the rank of a subject, his people should be constrained to take the oath of allegiance to Caesar, in place of the oath to Herod which they had formerly taken.[65] It was the practice under the empire that all subjects, both Romans and provincials, should swear allegiance and fidelity to the Emperor. In later time, under Trajan, the oath was taken every year on the anniversary of the Emperor›s accession, but it is uncertain when this custom was introduced. The words which Josephus uses would seem to imply that the oath to Caesar was taken and refused only once;[66] and the occasion is implied to have been towards the end of Herod›s life.

The two acts, the oath and the enrollment, obviously form part of the new policy of Augustus towards Herod, though we need not go so far as to suppose that the two were one (as some scholars have done), and that the oath was taken as part of the ceremony of enrollment.

Incidentally, we may notice as a masterpiece of irrationality and uncritical prejudice, the reflection which Strauss makes about the oath of allegiance to Augustus imposed on the Jews. "That this oath, far from being a humiliating measure for Herod, coincided with his interest, is proved by the zeal with which he punished the Pharisees who refused to take it."[67] Naturally, Herod had to punish the refusal as an act of treason. If he did not do so, any one of his enemies could ruin him by reporting the fact to Augustus. Moreover, there were so many Roman officials in Syria that the omission to punish the recalcitrants could not be kept from their knowledge, and every official was in duty bound to report the omission to his superiors or to the Emperor. The punishment, however, was very mild: a fine was inflicted on the whole 6000 recalcitrants, and was paid by the wife of Herod's brother Pheroras. Subsequently, the ringleaders were put to death; but that was not on account of their refusing the oath, but because they were disobedient and disrespectful to Herod himself on a later occasion.

Herod was, naturally, unwilling to accept this mark of servitude and degradation in rank without making an effort to avoid it. He would, doubtless, request time; and he would have little or no difficulty in obtaining leave from the Roman governor, Saturninus, to postpone the numbering, until he had sent an embassy to Rome. Herod had formerly had great influence with Augustus; he might become powerful again; and the Roman officials had no reason to refuse compliance with such a reasonable request for temporary delay. Herod could represent with perfect truth that the imposition of a Roman census in Palestine would offend the prejudices of the Jews, and endanger the peace of the kingdom. Moreover, the crafty king knew well how to make his requests acceptable to Roman officers, who were almost invariably accessible to bribery.

Further, according to Josephus, Herod's case was a good and strong one, and Syllaeus was a false accuser. After Saturninus had come to Syria as governor, in succession to Titius (probably in the summer of 9 BC. [68]), long negotiations went on in his presence between Herod and Syllaeus; an arrangement was made between them; it was afterwards broken by Syllaeus; Herod again complained to Saturninus, and was authorized to make war on the Arabians.

Incidentally, we notice that both the accusation that Herod had made war without Roman sanction, and the defense that he had been authorized by the governor of Syria, show how far he was from being an independent king.

It is, therefore, natural and probable that a postponement of the enrollment should have been granted to Herod; and, although our authorities merely say that an embassy was sent, and give no information as to the exact message, yet we may fairly assume that it was intended both to soothe the anger of Augustus and to beg for exemption from the enrollment, on the ground that this was likely to rouse the religious feeling of the Jews and cause disturbance and insurrection.

The embassy was sent to Rome, but it was not received in audience, and it returned without effecting anything. Augustus, of course, knew in a general way what instructions had been given to it, and he did not think that Herod had been sufficiently humiliated. Perhaps Herod's case was not quite so good as Josephus represents it, and there was something to be said on the Arabian side of which we are not informed. Augustus must assuredly have received the reports of Saturninus the governor, and of Volumnius his own procurator; but he still continued stern and unforgiving to Herod.

In these circumstances the delay granted to Herod in regard to the enrollment was not extended, and, as we may suppose, he was called upon to obey the emperor's orders. He sent a second embassy to Augustus, which was, in all probability, commissioned not, as before, to request exemption from the enrollment, but to announce his submission and to promise unconditional compliance. This embassy was much more favorably received, and returned from Rome successful; but Herod was evidently by no means completely pardoned or restored fully to favor. When once Augustus's anger had been roused at the Jewish monarch's assumption of too great freedom, it was far from easy to appease it entirely, and impossible to eradicate the effect produced on his mind.

The succession to Herod's kingdom was subject to the sanction of Augustus[69] He could not punish his own sons without formally accusing them before a council of his relatives and the Roman officers of the province.[70] He had to send embassy after embassy to Rome to obtain the sanction of Augustus for his intended acts. He could not punish his guilty son Antipater without getting special leave from Augustus. In fact his kingdom was treated ostentatiously as an outlying part of the province, in which nothing of any consequence could go on without the Roman sanction.

Luke's statement that the enrollment was applied to Palestine is therefore in perfect accord with the situation as revealed by Josephus during the last years of the life of Herod. The question that remains is: In what year was the enrollment made in Palestine?

The year which was generally observed in the southern part of the Province Syria and perhaps followed by Josephus in his history, began in the spring.[71] In Syria, therefore, the periodic year was probably 9-8 BC. and the actual numbering would take place in the year 8-7 BC.

The recital of events which has just been given will prove that the numbering in Palestine could not have occurred so early as the year 8-7, ending 17th April, 7 BC. A consideration of the character of the enrollment will bring us to a more precise result.

Herod was naturally eager to avoid giving to the enrollment an entirely foreign and non-national character Such a character both accentuated his own humiliation and was more liable to rouse the ever-wakeful pride and jealousy of his Jewish subjects. Obviously, the best way to soothe the Jewish sentiment was to give the enrollment a tribal character and to number the tribes of Israel, as had been done by purely national Governments.

PART II. Solution of the Problem

The Roman officials would not be likely to object to this form of enrollment. Provided Herod obeyed the orders of Augustus that an enrollment must be made, it would be entirely in accordance with the spirit in which these subject kingdoms were treated, that the manner of making the enrollment should be left to the discretion of the responsible authority, *viz*, the king. Moreover, the marvelous success of Roman provincial administration was due to the skill and tact with which the officials accommodated themselves to the prejudices of the subject population; and this was clearly a case in, which Jewish susceptibilities might be taken into account as regards the manner of numbering. The people was well known to be stubborn and unyielding in its religious ideas; and, with rare exceptions, Rome humored its religious prejudices.

In his work on the relations between the Imperial law and the National law, Dr. Mitteis has shown how much the Roman law was affected in the Eastern provinces by national law and custom.[72] In those countries Rome was brought in contact with an old civilization and a settled system of Greek law; and it did not seek to force on them its own law, as it did on the barbarous countries of the West. Similarly, the Roman governor of Syria was not likely to dictate the precise fashion in which the numbering of Palestine must be carried out.

Moreover, we have already seen that the prime consideration in the Imperial system of administering the provinces was to avoid disturbance and sedition. Augustus and the later emperors emphatically inculcated this principle on their lieutenants in the provinces. Herod could with perfect justice show that tribal numbering was the form which would tend most to peace and order in his kingdom.

Herod's method in governing his kingdom was, as we have seen, to humor the Jews, and to accept the distinction which they proudly drew between themselves and the heathen. Must we not, then, suppose that he would employ the same method in his enrollment? Owing to the care with which the Jews preserved their family records and pedigrees, all true Jews would know what was their family and their proper city according to the ancient tribal system, even though they might have been forced by circumstances to change their abode. This seems to have suggested the mode of enrollment which Luke describes a mode which would mark off by a broad clear line the true Jews from the mongrel population of Palestine. All who claimed to be Jews were to repair to the proper city of their tribe and family. The rest of the population, who were probably much more numerous, would be counted according to their ordinary place of residence.

My friend, Professor Paterson, to whom I am indebted throughout these pages, points out that Augustus would specially desire an enrollment of Palestine in order to have some clear idea what was the military strength of the country. It was a troublesome district to rule. Disturbances were always apprehended. There was obvious advantage in knowing what was the exact strength of the possible rebels.

Moreover, the non-Jewish population was peaceable and well-affected to Rome. The enrollment would obviously be much more useful, if in distinguished accurately the rebellious from the peaceful element in the population. The tribal enrollment furnished the means of gaining this information. It might safely be concluded that all those who were content to be counted as non-tribal would be loyal subjects of Rome. The imposition of the oath of allegiance to Augustus would also furnish a test, and the number of those who refused the oath was kept. Josephus says there were more than 6000. He implies, not that this was an estimate of the strength of the Pharisaic faction, but that those who actually refused to take the oath were counted; and he says that they were regarded as dangerous and likely to rouse war and disturbance.[73]

According to Luke the tribal enrollment was made by ordering every head of a household to repair for the numbering to the proper city from which his family had sprung. Such a method would have been entirely inapplicable in a large country. But, as the traveler rides across the length of Palestine, it is vividly brought home to him that this was an easy and short method in that land. The Romans, who required that citizens should travel to Rome from the remotest part of Italy when they wished to register their vote, would see nothing to object to, if Herod consulted them as to his proposed scheme.

In the national character which Herod gave to his enrollment, probably, lies the reason why Mary as well as Joseph went up to Bethlehem – a detail which would be so inexplicable if the enrollment had been modeled after a Roman census. To go personally to the enrollment was regarded as substantiating a claim to true Hebrew origin and family. All they that went to their proper city were true Hebrews; and, as Luke says, "all (*i.e.*, all true Hebrews in Palestine) went to enroll themselves, every one to his own city".

It is important to notice the force of the word "all" here. This is one of many passages in Luke's History where the precise sense that should be attributed to the word "all" or the word "they" may be, or has been, a subject of controversy, and can be determined only from the whole train of thought in the historian's mind. He that misconceives the general thought underlying the whole passage inevitably misinterprets "they" or "all"

For example, who are "they" in Acts 13:3? On the way in which that question is answered hinges a controversy as to Church government. Who are "all" in Acts 18:17? On the answer depends the whole sense of the incident; but an answer is difficult, and depends on the general conception in the reader's mind. Some say "all the Jews beat a Christian": others say "all the Greeks beat a Jew". Similarly, who are "us" in Luke 1:1? Professor Blass has recently answered that in his own way. Many would give a different reply.

Accordingly, to understand "all" in Luke 2:3, one must put oneself at the narrator's point of view. As we have seen, he conveys the impression throughout the two chapters that he is giving the story of Mary herself. To her "all" are the Jews: she thinks only of her own people: the nonJewish population of Palestine is not embraced in her view.

But, when such a plan of tribal numbering was adopted, the time of year had to be carefully considered. In the first place the winter months had to be avoided, during which traveling was often difficult, and in which unfavorable weather might cause great hardship and even prevent the plan from being carried out. As the day had to be fixed a long time beforehand, it must have been fixed in the season when good weather could be calculated on. In winter, weather might be good or it might be bad, and at the best it would be cold and trying.

That a day was fixed by the authorities, and that it was not left to the discretion of the people to go when they pleased (as in Egypt people seem to have been permitted to send in their enrollment papers at any time they pleased within the year), seems to follow from the fact that Joseph and Mary traveled from Nazareth to Bethlehem at the very time when the birth of the child was approaching. Moreover, the advantages of the plan in ease and speed would have been sacrificed, unless a day had been fixed for the numbering.

Further, it was urgently necessary that the time which was fixed should not interfere with agricultural operations – that it should not come between the earliest date for the first harvest and the latest date for finishing the threshing, and getting in the grain and the fine cut straw from the threshing floors.[74] The harvest varied considerably in different parts of the country, and reaping extended over about seven weeks, beginning from the middle of April.

Taking these circumstances into consideration, we may say with considerable confidence that August to October is the period within which the numbering would be fixed. It is no objection to this view that tradition places the birth of Jesus at Christmas. It is well known that the tradition is not early, that it varies in different periods and in different sections of the Church, and that the earliest belief was different.

Lewin, in *Fasti Sacri*, p. 115, selects 1st August as the day and month. Without laying any stress on the reasoning from the priestly periods by which he reaches this precise and exact conclusion, we must attach great weight to the argument which he founds on the fact that the shepherds were watching their flocks in the open country by night. In Asia Minor, at least, the pasturing of the flocks by night takes place only during the hot season and not in the winter. The sheep will not eat under the hot sun: they stand idly in a dense crowd in any place where the semblance of shade can be found during the day, and during the night they scatter and feed. In cold weather they seek food during the day.

On this characteristic of the sheep is founded the rule, said to be observed in Palestine, that the flocks were sent out after the Passover and brought in about October before the "former rain".

Within that period, April to October, the day fixed for the numbering must fall; and during that period April to July was required for the reaping and garnering of the year's crop.

It seems unnecessary to do more than refer to the idle objection that has been made: How were the shepherds numbered? There must always be some people for whom the numbering is inconvenient, whatever be the time at which it is fixed; and we need not trouble to inquire what was the method adopted to meet the special case of the shepherds. That inquiry belongs to the sphere of the archaeological student, who studies the *minutiæ* of the census system; but the historian, in his more general view, must omit such details. No critic, who retains his sober reason and does not yield to mere prejudice, would find any difficulty in it.

After all, not a great deal of journeying to and fro would be required for the enrollment. The remnant that could trace their origin to the Ten Tribes must have been very small. The majority of the strictly Jewish population was probably resident at that time in the southern part of Palestine, though there was also a large minority scattered over all the cities of the central and northern districts. A considerable number of people would have to make journeys of one to four days to their own city, and the same back again; but nothing approaching to a general transference of population would be necessitated.

For Herod's enrollment, then, there is open only the late summer of 7 or 6 BC. Unless we have omitted some important factor (which is, of course, far from improbable, considering how scanty the evidence is), the enrollment can hardly be brought down so late as 5 BC. and we have seen that 8 BC. is excluded by other considerations.

Between the years 7 and 6 it is difficult to choose, so long as we confine ourselves to the evidence outside of Luke, for that evidence is insufficient to found a judgment upon, owing to the uncertainty of all the dates connected with the question. It may be that the embassy which was dismissed unheard by Augustus, returned so late that the necessary preparations and notice could not be made in time for the autumn of 7 BC. and it is certain that Herod was by no means eager to hurry the numbering. But these are mere vague presumptions.

Luke, however, gives additional information about the Savior's life, which affords reasonable confidence that 6 BC. was the year of Christ's birth.

NOTE

That a difference should be made in the treatment of Jews and non-Jews in Palestine, is quite in accordance with Roman usage. For example, after the rebellion under Hadrian, the Jews were forbidden to enter Jerusalem.

---

[63] Dr. Schuerer well describes the ambiguous policy of Herod, *Gesch. d. Jud. Volkes, etc.*, 2., p. 327 f.

[64] πάλαι χρώμενος αὐτῷ φίλῳ, νῦν ὑπηκόῳ χρήσεται, Josephus, *Ant. Jud.*, 16., 9, 3 (§ 290).

[65] Schuerer, *l. c.*, 1., p. 329; Josephus, 15., 10, 4.

[66] παντὸς γοῦν τοῦ Ἰουδαϊκοῦ βεβαιώσαντος δι' ὅρκων ἦ μὴν εὐνοήσειν Καίσαρι . . . οἵδε οὐκ ὤμοσαν. Josephus, *Ant. Jud.*, 17., 2, 4. The aorists imply a single occasion, not a regularly repeated custom.

[67] *Life of Jesus*, 1., p. 203.

[68] Some date his arrival as late as 8 BC. This would make the delay in the enrollment of Judea all the more natural. He was succeeded by Quinctilius Varus in 7. See Note 1 at end of chapter 11.

[69] *Ant. Jud.*, 17., 3, 2 (§ 53); 8, 2 (§ 195).

[70] τῶν κατὰ τὴν ἐπαρχίαν ἡγεμόνων *Bell. Jud.*, 1., 27, 1.

[71] See Niese in *Hermes*, 28., 1893, p. 212 ff.; also see Notes at the end of chapter 10.

[72] *Reichsrecht und Volksrecht*, Leipzig, 1891.

[73] ἐκ τοῦ προὔπτου εἰς τὸ πολεμεῖν τε καὶ βλάπτειν ἐπηρμένοι, *Ant. Jud.*, 17., 2, 4 (41).

[74] See Mr. J. W. Paterson›s excellent article on «Agriculture» in Hastings› *Dictionary of the Bible*. On the use of the fine chopped straw in the economy of the farm, see *Contemporary Review*, August, 1897, p. 237.

Chapter 10.
CHRONOLOGY OF THE LIFE OF CHRIST

LUKE 3:23 tells that Jesus appeared before the world as the teacher, when he was about thirty years of age. Now it is a characteristic usage in Greek to employ this vague expression, when there is no intention to imply doubt as to the age: it lies in the genius of the language to avoid positiveness in assertion, and to prefer less definite and pronounced and harsh forms of statement.[75] It is unnecessary to think that Luke was really doubtful what was the age of Jesus, whether twenty-eight or thirty-two. His elaborately careful and precise dating, 3:1, 2, may be taken as an indication that he had good and accurate information on the subject; that he «had investigated all the circumstances accurately in their origin». But, like a true Greek, he says «about thirty,» where the less sensitive barbarian of our northern island would use a rudely positive and definite number. The only doubt that remains is whether Luke means in his thirtieth year, or when he was thirty years old; and this doubt is resolved by the other facts recorded by Luke, as we shall see. Jesus was thirty years old, when he began his public career.

The precise statement is doubtless derived from the same authority as the whole of the first two chapters (and perhaps also 4:16-30); and the only reason for recording it is that it was given exactly by a first-rate authority, and therefore helped Luke's readers "to know the certainty concerning the things wherein they had been instructed". An authority, who was really good on such a point, would know the exact age, and Luke expressly declares his intention of setting down only such facts as he had accurately and certainly on trustworthy authority. Where his knowledge was only vague, he usually refrains from making any statement.

If the birth of Jesus occurred in BC. 6, he became thirty years of age in the second half of AD. 25, and his appearance as a teacher took place within the year that followed. If his birth occurred in BC. 7, the date of his appearance must be placed one year earlier, but we shall find reason to reject that supposition.

Some time, but apparently quite a short time, before Jesus came forward as a teacher, John the Baptist began to preach that the Messiah was at hand; and Jesus was among the crowds who flocked to him to receive baptism. Now, as Luke mentions, "the word of God came to John" in the fifteenth year of the authority[76] of Tiberius Caesar. The date is given very precisely and definitely; but, unfortunately, it is by no means easy to say what year is meant by it.

It is often found that, where an ancient writer aims at making his statement most precise and exact, his words lend themselves to several interpretations.[77] What did Luke understand by the authority of Tiberius? In the inscriptions of that emperor›s lifetime, the years of his reign are estimated according to the number of times that he had received tribunician power. On that system his fifteenth year began on 27th June, AD. 13. Obviously Luke cannot intend that year.

Again, according to Velleius, the admirer and friend and faithful follower of Tiberius, associated with him in nine years of warfare, authority equal to that of Augustus in all the provinces and armies of the empire was granted to Tiberius by the senate and people, on the proposal of Augustus himself, before he returned to Rome to celebrate his triumph over the peoples of Pannonia and Dalmatia. Now this triumph was celebrated on 16th January, AD. 12,[78] therefore the decree of equal power must have been passed before the end of AD. 11. Further, the language of Velleius suggests that the decree was issued not long before Tiberius returned, and it was so closely connected with his return that Suetonius seems to place it after he reached Rome. But Velleius›s authority must be ranked superior in regard to such a point.

There can be no doubt that this was the event which Tacitus had ill mind when he said that Tiberius had been created *Collega Imperii* during the lifetime of Augustus (*Annals*, 1., 3).

It follows that the first year during which Tiberius held power as colleague of Augustus with equal power in all provinces of the empire

PART II. Solution of the Problem

coincided with the end of AD. 11 and the greater part of AD. 12, and the fifteenth year with AD. 25-6. [79]

If Luke counted the years of Tiberius according to that system, all his statements as to time in these early chapters are found to be consistent and accurate. The first enrollment must have taken place in autumn BC. 6. Jesus was thirty years old in autumn BC. 25. In the later months of that year, when the fifteenth year of the *Hegemonia* of Tiberius in the provinces had just recently begun (according to the official usage[80]), John appeared announcing the coming of Christ; and very shortly thereafter Jesus came and was baptized by John in the river Jordan. A month or two thereafter occurred the Passover on 21st March, AD. 26 (Lewin, *Fasti Sacri*, p. 173).

The only reason for doubting whether Luke could have counted the years of Tiberius on that system, is that it is never employed elsewhere in reckoning the reign of that emperor. When his tribunician years are not stated, his reign is always elsewhere counted from the death of his predecessor, Augustus; and it is beyond dispute that he was not in any proper and strict sense emperor until that time. But it seems not impossible that his *Hegemonia* in the provinces might be counted from AD. 11, when his authority began in them. Similarly, we saw that in Egypt the reign of Augustus was reckoned, not from any date when he became emperor in a strict and proper sense, but from BC. 30, when his authority began in that country.

Further, Luke, the whole spirit of whose History stamps it as belonging to the Flavian period, knew that the reign of Titus was counted from the day when he was made the colleague of his father, Vespasian; and thus he may have been led to apply to the time of Tiberius the principle which was in current and official use while he was writing.[81]

Now the only dates that are permissible for the crucifixion are AD. 29, 30 and 33. Different authorities vary between these three years. But, as it is not possible to allow that more than four Passovers occurred during the public career of Jesus, we are bound to the view that his career extended from the time preceding the Passover of 26 till the Passover of 29. The strength of the tradition that places the crucifixion in

29 has been admirably stated by Mr. C. H. Turner in his article on the "Chronology of the New Testament".[82]

But is this consistent with Luke's narrative? Does he permit the supposition that four Passovers occurred within the period of Jesus' teaching?

Luke does not refer to any Passover during that whole period except the last. He was not interested in the relation of Jesus to the Jewish feasts, and hardly alludes to the subject after the Passover that occurred in the Savior's twelfth year. Hence we cannot expect from him much direct evidence bearing on the Passovers during the teaching of Jesus.

Moreover, Luke had little of the sense for chronology, the value of which in clearly understanding or describing any series of incidents had not been appreciated so early as the first century. Chronology, too, was much more difficult when no era had come into general use, when dates were commonly stated by the names of annual magistrates, or the years of sovereigns, and when in Asia scores of different eras for dating had just begun to come into use side by side with one another, so that, even when one does find a date by a numbered year, it is often a difficult problem to determine what era is used.

Want of chronological sense or interest may seem a serious defect in a historian. But we are too apt to forget that Luke was not writing for us, and that he was not even writing for posterity. He wrote for the benefit of his own contemporaries. His work stands in the closest relation to the time. That which seemed most important for the requirements of the Church at the time was what Luke most desired to record with absolute accuracy and trustworthiness. Abstract scientific interest in the chronology of the Gospel did not exist among his readers. What they were concerned with was its truth; and that was gathered from the Savior's teaching, from his statements about himself, and from the facts of his Birth, Death and Resurrection. These were the points on which Luke's attention was concentrated in his first book.

Some authorities are disposed to think that Luke believed the whole period of the teaching of Jesus to have been comprised within the period of a little more than a year, lasting from shortly before one Passover till

PART II. Solution of the Problem

the Passover of the following year. A widely-spread opinion in the second and third centuries assigned that duration to the Savior's ministry, but I can discover nothing to show that Luke shared it. The opinion, probably, was the result of two causes. In the first place, the notes of time in the Gospels are very slight and difficult to fit together. In the second place, the saying about "the acceptable year of the Lord" was easily misunderstood.

The memory of the earliest authorities, as a rule, was entirely filled with the words and teaching of the Savior. Chronological order was little thought of; and we should probably find that most of the writings alluded to by Luke 1. I took the form of collections of sayings and parables. The only events, probably, that were vividly remembered in their historical aspect and apart from the doctrine connected with them, were the series of actions comprised within the last few days of the Savior's life. The sequence of these events was indelibly stamped on the memory of all.[83] But the rest of the tradition was a reproduction of past lessons and impressive sayings. These were connected with certain localities; some were associated with certain actions of the Savior or of those who were in his company. But his numerous journeys great and small were not remembered in their sequence. In this state of information, Luke evidently forbore the attempt to describe exactly the movements of Jesus during the greater part of the teaching.

In the beginning, indeed, he describes the sequence of Jesus' first journeys. He tells how Jesus was baptized by John in Jordan, 3:21; and he dates at that point the beginning of his teaching, 3:23. Then he tells of the journey into the wilderness, *i.e.*, the country south from Jerusalem, and mentions that Jesus was actually in Jerusalem, 4:1-13. Thereafter Jesus returned to Galilee and taught there for some time, 4:14, 15, after which he returned to Nazareth for a brief visit, 4:16-30. Being rejected and threatened with death at Nazareth, he came down to Capernaum, 4:31.

The narrative during this stage touches that of the other Gospels at occasional points; and one paragraph, 4:1-13, is perhaps founded on the same ultimate authority as Matthew 4:1-11 (though with a difference in order). No indication of the lapse of time is given; but some considerable period is likely to have elapsed even in the events implied in 4:15 alone.

But at this point, 4:31, begins a new section of the narrative. The indications of movement for a considerable period are of the vaguest kind. 4:42, He went into a desert place. 5:16, He withdrew himself in the deserts. 5:27, He went forth. 6:1, He was going through the cornfields, probably in May or June when the wheat was ripe but not cut. 6:12, He went out into the mountain to pray. 6:17, He came down with them. 7:1, He entered into Capernaum. 7:1, He went soon afterwards to a city called Nain (an episode peculiar to Luke). His return from Nain is never mentioned, but 7:18 ff. probably belongs to the coasts of the Sea of Galilee. 8:1, He soon afterwards went about through cities and villages. 8:22, He entered into a boat (on the Sea of Galilee). 8:26, He arrived at the country of the Gerasenes, which is over against Galilee. 8:38, He entered into a boat and returned. 9:10, He withdrew apart to a city called Bethsaida. 9:28, He went up about eight days after into the mountain to pray. 9:37, On the next day when they were come down from the mountain, a great multitude met him (and here Mark's reference to the green grass, 6:39, and John's to the abundant grass, 6:10, show that the time was spring).

In this part of the narrative, the lapse of time is hardly alluded to: only the brief and vague indications just quoted are given. The marks of locality, apart from those implied in the indications of movement, are also very vague and elusive. 4:44, He was preaching in the synagogues of Galilee. 5:1, He was standing by the Lake of Gennesaret. 5:12, He was in one of the cities.

This section of the narrative, 4:31-9:50, is as a whole (though with some considerable exceptions) closely parallel to Mark and Matthew. Great part of the section is evidently founded on an authority common to them (though we expressly avoid stating any opinion as to the nature of the connection between the three).

It is plain that though Luke, with his usual indifference to the chronological aspect of history, does not properly mark the lapse of time, yet this section must extend over some considerable period.

PART II. Solution of the Problem

"Preaching in the synagogues of Galilee" is the sort of phrase by which Luke sums up a considerable period; and the different movements, mentioned or implied, vague as they are, together with the intervals between them, demand time.

From 9:51 begins another new section describing the movement to Jerusalem preparatory to the culmination of Christ's teaching there. In 10:38, as they went on their way, he entered into a certain village (*viz.*, Bethany); and in 11:1, he was praying in a certain place. In this and the following chapters there continues the same vagueness. Luke only makes it clear that the most advanced stage in the ministry has begun, and that Jesus is moving gradually towards the south and is affecting the southern half of Palestine. In 13:22, he went on his way through towns and villages teaching and journeying on unto Jerusalem. In 17:11, as they were on the way to Jerusalem, he was passing through the midst of Samaria and Galilee. 8:31, We go up to Jerusalem. 18:35, He drew nigh unto Jericho. 19:1, He entered and was passing through Jericho. 19:11, He was nigh to Jerusalem. 19:28 f., He went on before, going up to Jerusalem (by the steep road from Jericho), and he drew nigh to Bethany.

Then comes the entry into Jerusalem, where the rest of the narrative has its scene.

With very slight exceptions, the section 9:51-19:28 is quite peculiar to Luke, and has hardly any points of contact with any of the other Gospels. But the same vagueness of place and time continues.

It is, however, clearly unnecessary and improbable that this section represents, or was considered by Luke to represent, the events of one single continuous approximately straight journey. The multitudes, the towns and villages, the frequent repetition of the idea of progress towards Jerusalem, imply a gradual advance of the circle of the teaching towards the south and towards the center of Jewish religion and the completion of his mission.

If, as I believe to be probably the case, Luke knew what was the "certain village" of Martha and Mary, 10:38, but for some reason (about which we need not speculate) avoided naming it, our view would be raised to complete certainty, that in this section the historian is describing a general movement southwards, accompanied and complicated by many short journeys to and fro, up and down, "through towns and villages teaching". If he is at Bethany in 10., and at Jericho in 18, and in Samaria in 17, zigzag wanderings are clearly implied. But, as many may prefer to consider that 10:38 has been put in false local and chronological order by Luke through his ignorance that the "certain village" was Bethany, we need not press an argument that is not actually required for our purpose. Even without it the view which we are stating as to Luke's intention in this section seems certain.

It is obvious, then, that Luke divides the teaching of Jesus, previous to the final scenes in Jerusalem, into three stages. The first and preliminary stage – in the wilderness of Judah, in Galilee and in Nazareth – is very briefly recorded The second – spent in Galilee or the north continuously – is described at much greater length: Jesus had now become a famous teacher, and attracted many hearers and followers. The third – the extension of the sphere of influence over central Palestine as Far as Jerusalem – is described still more fully. There is no attempt or intention to describe the movements of Jesus exactly in the second and third stages.

Further, the second stage evidently lasted a Full year, For after it has begun some time, we find ourselves in the month of May or June, and at the end we are again in spring (as we know From Mark but not from Luke).

The probability, then, is that roughly the three stages correspond to the three years; and the memory of the witnesses retained very little that was accurate and definite (except some important changes of scene and journeys) during the preliminary stage, AD. 26, more about the second, AD. 27, and still more about the third, AD. 28.

The first Passover, AD. 26 (John 2:13), falls about Luke 4:13, and the year ends about 4:31. At the feast of this year, the Jews spoke about the 46th year of the building of the Temple (John 2:20); and the 46th year had begun shortly before they spoke.[84]

The second Passover, AD. 27 (John 5:1), falls about Luke 5. Then follows the month of May, 6:1.

PART II. Solution of the Problem

The spring of AD. 28 and the third Passover (John 6:4) must be placed in Luke 9. The summer of this year, however, was still spent in Galilee, according to John 7:1; but it is not inconsistent with this statement that the third stage of Luke had already begun. The characteristic of that stage was that Jesus had now set his face firmly to go to Jerusalem, 9:51; but during it, he was still passing through the midst of Samaria and Galilee, 17:11. The period in Luke's estimation is rather one of firm and definite resolution than of bodily movement continuously towards Jerusalem. The visit to the country east of Jordan (Mark 10:1 and Matthew 19:1) certainly belongs to this stage.

That there was a strong tradition to the effect that the Savior suffered at the age of thirty-three seems to follow from the agreement of Hippolytus[85] and Eusebius and Phlegon. The latter, as is allowed by Mr. Turner, was indebted to very early Christian authorities for his information. It is true that both Eusebius and Phlegon place the crucifixion in AD. 33, but this arises from their both depending on the original Christian calculation which ultimately gave rise to the modern era of the birth of Christ. This was wrongly calculated as early as the second century; and, starting from that initial error, the chronologists had to place the beginning of the teaching in thirty and the crucifixion in thirty-three.

It is a strong confirmation of our result that it agrees with two so ancient traditions, which are quite unconnected with one another and evidently seemed to most of the ancients to be inconsistent with each other.

Starting from a very different point of view from that of Mr. Turner, and working on utterly diverse lines, we have reached nearly the same conclusion that he reached. The only differences of importance are two: –

1. I find myself obliged, on the principles of interpretation which I have followed consistently throughout, to attach a distinctly higher value than he does to Luke's statement as to the age of Jesus when he began to teach.

2. Mr. Turner is inclined to think that Luke compressed the teaching into one year; and he holds that the teaching in reality lasted only for

two years, interpreting John 5:1 as referring to some unnamed minor feast.[86] This view cannot be disproved, but it seems to have nothing to recommend it, and it introduces quite unnecessary discord between the different Gospels. The chronological marks in the Gospels are so slight that almost anything can be made out of them, if one is bent on doing so. Hence there was in ancient time an immense variety of opinion on this point. But in four independent accounts of one series of events, a reasonable criticism will prefer the interpretation in which all the various conditions are reconciled.

At the last moment, after this chapter is in type, Professor Paterson reminds me that the result which we have attained agrees with the celebrated calculation of Kepler, who fixed on the year BC. 6, because in March of that year there occurred a conjunction of Jupiter, Saturn and Mars, which would present a most brilliant appearance in the sky, and would naturally attract the attention of observers interested in the phenomena of the heavens, as were the Wise Men of the East.

I have no knowledge what is the value of Kepler's reckoning. Mr. Turner, who knows much more about the matter, speaks only of the conjunction of Jupiter and Saturn, which occurred in, May, October and December, BC. 7; and I presume that he would have mentioned the triple conjunction (on which Kepler laid such stress), if he had accepted the calculation, even though it does not suit the date 7-6, to which he inclines. The coincidence, however, seems worthy of mention, but it is not presented as an argument.

But, while we lay no stress upon it as an argument, the subject is so interesting, and presents so many curious coincidences, that a few paragraphs may profitably be devoted to it.

The conjunction of Jupiter and Saturn in the constellation Pisces, according to a Jewish belief of some antiquity,[87] is the sign of the Messiah›s coming. If there existed some belief that the coming of a King of the Jews was to be heralded thus, the occurrence of the phenomenon would necessarily arrest the attention of the astrology-loving priests in the East. Kepler›s theory was, that just as the conjunction in 1604 of Jupiter and Saturn, culminated in 1605 in the conjunction of Jupiter,

Saturn and Mars, and was followed by the appearance of a new and brilliant star, which disappeared again after about eighteen months, so in BC. 7 and 6, the exactly singular conjunctions were followed by the appearance of a new star after the triple conjunction, and that this was the star of Matthew 2:2.

Now the visit of the Magi obviously did not occur until more than forty days after the birth of Jesus,[88] and may probably be placed during the winter of BC. 6-5. Kepler›s theory involves that they appeared before Herod at this time, and informed him of the reason of their coming. Herod thereupon consulted the Jewish priests, and heard from them that the King was to be born in Bethlehem. He also questioned the Magi privately, and learned the exact facts with regard to the appearance of the star, and doubtless also with regard to the whole phenomenon in the heavens. He would learn from the Magi that the fateful conjunction first occurred in May of the year BC. 7. Then he sent the Magi away to Bethlehem, and awaited news of their discovery. When they did not return, he ordered all children under two years of age in Bethlehem to be killed. The King might have been born at any time after the first conjunction occurred; and that was at least eighteen months ago. Therefore, in order to make sure, the order included every child under two.

Now about this time, as Josephus mentions,[89] Herod was troubled by a prophecy that the power was about to pass away from him and from his family; and the Pharisees, from favor to the wife of Pheroras (who promised to pay their fine), predicted that the succession would come to her and her children. Obviously, the second part of the prophecy was pure invention, due to partisanship; but the first part was almost certainly connected with the Jews› deep-seated belief in the coming of a new King, the Messiah. Lewin (whose arrangement of the events in the last three years of Herod›s life seems very good) places this event in BC. 6; Schuerer dates it in 7. One or the other must be right. Herod put to death the ringleaders of the Pharisees, with two of his own personal attendants, and also all those of his own household that had associated themselves with the prediction of the Pharisees.

There occurred therefore a number of deaths among the family and attendants of Herod in connection with the belief in the coming of a new King.

Now Macrobius, a pagan writer about AD. 400, says that when the news was brought to Augustus that Herod, King of the Jews, had ordered children under two years of age in Syria to be slain, and that among them was a son of Herod's, the Emperor remarked, "It is better to be Herod's pig than his son".[90] It is not probable that Macrobius was indebted to a Christian writer for this story;[91] and, therefore, probably the story of the Massacre of the Infants was recorded in some pagan source. The execution of the conspirators in Herod›s household perhaps occurred about the same time; but among them there is not likely to have been a son of Herod›s. Only a few months before, however, Herod had put to death two of his sons, and the remark of Augustus may have been prompted by hearing successively of so many barbarities, the execution of two sons, of a number of infants, and of several of his own family and personal attendants.

While all these statements furnish only vague presumptions, yet they certainly tend to show that much was going on of a remarkable character about BC. 7-6, and they fit in well with both Luke and Matthew. If the narratives of these two writers are true, they throw much light on Josephus and Macrobius, and receive illustration and confirmation from them.

But that which is most certain is that our non-Christian authorities are most meager and fragmentary. It is the extreme of uncritical and unscholarly procedure to condemn the Christian authorities because they tell some things which are not mentioned in any non-Christian source.

NOTE 1

The fifteenth year of Tiberius. There are various ways of counting the years of an emperor's reign; and doubt often exists which way is intended, when a date is given.

Luke might reckon the years of an emperor as beginning always from the anniversary of the day on which power was conferred on him.

That mode of reckoning seems to have been always used by the emperors of the first century. In that case the fifteenth year of Tiberius's rule in the provinces began near the end of AD. 25, on the anniversary of the day when he originally received collegiate authority in the provinces. But that method was rarely, if ever, used by the general public or by historians in the East.

There was, however, a different method which was usually employed by many historians and chronologists, and was officially used by the emperors of the second and third centuries. The first year of the emperor was estimated to run from the day on which he assumed power to the conclusion of the current year; then the second year of the emperor began on the first day of the following current year.

If that reckoning was followed by Luke, we should have to inquire what system of years he followed, whether he counted the years as beginning on the Roman system from 1st January, or on the most usual Greek system in the Aegean lands from 23rd September, or on a common Syrian system from 18th April.[92] On these three systems the fifteenth year of Tiberius might begin either 1st January, BC. 25, or 23rd September, 25, or 18th April, 25.

But according to every system it will be found that the first Passover of Jesus' teaching was the Passover of AD. 26: the only difference which they make to the reckoning is that John's preaching might be made to begin a little earlier on some than on other systems.

NOTE 2

It is unfortunate that, in his admirable article on the "Chronology of the New Testament," Mr. C. H. Turner sometimes disregards the principle admitted by most of the recent chronologists – that when any event was taken as an era, the years were not reckoned beginning from that day, but the year 1 was reckoned as the current year within which the event occurred, as for example in the Asian year beginning 23rd September, the year 1 of the Actian era was the year *ending* 22nd September, B. C. 31, although the battle of Actium was fought as late as 2nd September, 31 (so that the year 1 of this era came to an end three weeks after it began). This principle has been proved repeatedly in the last few years, and many difficulties, formerly found in reckoning ancient dates, disappear as soon as it is applied. Mr. Turner follows the old method, that the year 1 runs for twelve months from the epoch-making event (*e.g.*, that the first year of Herod's reign lasted for 365 days from the day of his accession, and so on). Thus he is beset by the difficulties that result from it: *e.g.*, he declares that Josephus contradicts himself when he says that Antigonus died "on the day of the Great Fast in the consulship of Agrippa and Gallus (BC. 37), twenty-seven years to a day since the entry of Pompey into Jerusalem in the consulship of Antonius and Cicero (BC. 63)". Josephus, indeed, has admitted not a few faults and slips into his historical works; but it is surely going too far to say that the two reckonings given in this sentence contradict one another. There is no contradiction, if one counts like Josephus. According to Mr. Turner's reckoning, the lapse of twenty-seven years after (*circa*) 30th September, 63, brings us to 30th September, 36, but it brought Josephus only to 30th September, 37; and his two statements (made side by side in his text) agree exactly.

According to Niese in *Hermes*, 1893, p. 208 ff., Josephus in reckoning the years under the Roman emperors employed a solar year of the Julian type, but reckoned according to a Tylian (and perhaps common Syrian) method so that the year began from I Xanthicus, 18th April. Josephus also, as Niese holds, in order to avoid making the last year of one emperor coincide with the first year of his successor, reckoned the final year of each emperor as continuing, to the end of the current year, and made the first year of his successor begin only on 18th April following his accession. This was necessary if the years of the emperors were to be used in a continuous chronological system. In this way, the year 1 of Tiberius began on 18th April, AD. 15, and the year 22 continued to run till 17th April, AD. 37 (though the reign really lasted from 19th August, A.D. 14, to 16th March, AD. 37, *i.e.*, twenty-two years, six months, twenty-eight days). Similarly, the year 1 of Nero began only on 18th April, AD. 55, full six months after he really began to reign.

PART II. Solution of the Problem

Mr, Turner points out that Eusebius followed a similar (but not identical) method, counting the years of every emperor from the September after his succession.

Orosius either employed a reckoning of this character or was misled by some authority who did so; and hence he makes the tenth year of Claudius include an event that happened in 51, and we must suppose that he means the fourth year of Claudius to be AD. 45, and the ninth, AD. 50 (see *St. Paul the Traveller,* pp. 68, 254, where I did not perceive what was the explanation of Orosius's statements and called them errors).

But it is clear that Josephus did not employ this kind of reckoning for the Jewish rulers before Christ. It is more probable that he used either the Jewish sacred year beginning 1st Nisan (usually some time in March) or the Roman year beginning 1st January. For our purposes it will make no difference which system we follow (though there are, of course, many cases in which it might make the difference of a year); and as it will be simpler to use the Roman and modern reckoning from 1st January, we shall show the dates on that system.

1. Herod's reign *de jure* began from a decree of the Senate passed in the consulship of Domitius and Pollio BC. 40, during the 184th Olympiad which ended at midsummer in that year. Year 1 of Herod›s reign *de jure* ended on 31st December BC.. 40: year 37 of Herod's reign *de jure* ended on 31st December, BC. 4.

(If the decree was passed at a Senate meeting of 1st January or 1st February, and the Jewish reckoning from 1st Nisan be followed, the years of Herod's reign would all be carried back one year, so that the year 37 would end on 18th April, BC 4; but it is improbable that the decree was passed at these first two Senate meetings.) Herod died in the thirty seventh year of his reign *de jure, i.e.,* in the year BC. 4, immediately before the Passover, and perhaps (as Lewin reckons) on 1st April.

2. Pompey entered Jerusalem on the Great Fast about the end of September, BC. 63. In reckoning from this event, year 1 is the year ending 31st December, BC. 63; year 27 is the year ending 31st December, BC. 37; Herod succeeded as *de facto* king on the same fast day, twenty-seven years after Pompey entered Jerusalem, *i.e.,* about the end

of September, BC. 37, in which year the consuls were Agrippa and Gallus. Year 1 of Herod's reign *de facto* ended 31st December, BC. 37; year 18 of Herod's reign *de facto* ended 31st December, BC. 29; year 34 of Herod›s reign *de facto* ended 31st December, BC. 4.

Herod died in the year 34 of his reign *de facto, i.e.*, in the year BC. 4. This agrees exactly with the previous result.

Now the Temple began to be built in the eighteenth year of Herod, *i.e.*, BC. 20. In reckoning from this event (John 2:20), the Jews would presumably count according to their own system of sacred years beginning 1st Nisan. There is therefore a doubt what was the first year of the building of the Temple. If the building began in January-March, BC. 20, the first year would end at 1st Nisan 20, and would begin from 1st Nisan, BC. 21; but if the building began in April or later, the first year would end at 1st Nisan in BC. 19. We take the latter as more probable. Then the year 1 of the building of the Temple begins on 1st Nisan, BC. 20; year 46 of the building of the Temple begins on 1st Nisan, AD. 26.

The Jews disputing with Jesus at the Passover in the middle of Nisan AD. 26 would therefore on their system of reckoning call it the 46th year. "Forty and six years has this temple been in course of building (and is still building)."[93]

It is apparent how many uncertainties are caused in ancient chronology, through the variety of systems of reckoning the year, and other variations in different cities. We have not indicated nearly all such causes of doubt. For example, as M. Clermont Ganneau says, the Seleucid era was reckoned from 1st October, BC. 312, but the era of Damascus was reckoned from 23rd March of the same year.

NOTE 3

A different explanation of Luke's chronology may be approved by some, and it therefore deserves a place here. I am not aware that it has been advocated; but in all probability it has found some supporters, like every other possible view on this subject.

It is founded on the theory – which some think highly probable – that Luke considered the teaching of Jesus to have extended only over

PART II. Solution of the Problem

a little more than twelve months, beginning shortly before the Passover in one year and ending with the Passover of the following year. On that theory one might interpret the fifteenth year of Tiberius's reign in the usual way, from his assumption of power after the death of Augustus, 19th August, AD. 14. If, as many historians did, Luke reckoned the first year of Tiberius to end on 31st December, AD. 14, and the fifteenth year to begin 1st January, AD. 28, the baptism of Jesus would have to be placed early in that year, and the crucifixion at the Passover of 29. If, on the other hand, he reckoned the first year of Tiberius from 19th August, AD. 14, to 18th August, AD. 15, then the baptism of Jesus would have to be placed early in 29, and the crucifixion in AD. 30; but we have already set aside this supposition as less probable.

According to this method of explanation it would be necessary to suppose that in 3:23 Luke depended on an excellent authority, who knew both the correct age when Jesus began his teaching and the fact that the teaching lasted three years and a few months; but in 3:1-2 he depended on his own reckoning, founded on his false impression that the teaching lasted only one year and a few months. The fact would remain clear and certain that the crucifixion took place in AD. 29, and the teaching really began in the early spring of 26 (exactly as we have placed them).

There seems to us to be no necessity for supposing this partial error on Luke's part.

[75] The less definite form is strictly correct: Jesus was thirty years and a few months, more or less.
[76] *Hegemonia*, ἡγεμονία, is the word; on its sense see Chapter 11.
[77] Mommsen quotes a remarkable case in the *Monumentum Ancyranum* where Augustus›s desire to be precise and certain has exposed his statement of a number to be interpreted in three different ways by different writers.
[78] *Prosopographia Imp. Rom.*, 2., p. 183; Mommsen, *Staatsrecht*, 2., p 1159.
[79] See Note at end of chapter 10.
[80] See Note at end of chapter 10.
[81] See Mr. Turner in Dr. Hastings› *Dict. of Bible*, 1., p. 406.
[82] In Dr. Hastings› *Dict. of Bible*.
[83] Yet compare John 12:1 and Mark 14:1. See Note at the end of Chapter 4.
[84] See Note 2 at the end of Chapter 10.
[85] On Hippolytus see Mr. Turner›s remarks, *l. c.* p. 413, col. 2.

[86] Reading «a feast» instead of «the feast» (ἑορτὴ for ἡ ἑορτή).
[87] Mr. Turner says: «The statement of a medieval Jew, R. Abarbanel, that the conjunction of these two planets in Pisces is to be a sign of Messiah's coming, may perhaps have been derived ultimately from ancient traditions known to the Chaldaeans".
[88] The ceremony in Jerusalem, Luke 2:22, could not have taken place after the visit of the Magi, for the flight into Egypt must have followed immediately on the visit.
[89] *Ant. Jud.*, 17., 2, 4.
[90] Augustus must have uttered the witticism in Greek: the pun ((ὖν ἠυιόν) is lost in Latin or English: see Macrobius, *Sat.*, 2., 4.
[91] (1) The pagans of that time were strongly prejudiced against Christians and not likely to quote them. (2) A Christian author would have spoken about Palestine, not about Syria.
[92] See below, Note 2.
[93] See Mr. Turner on his p. 405.

PART II. Solution of the Problem

Chapter 11.
QUIRINIUS THE GOVERNOR OF SYRIA

WE come now to the last serious difficulty in Luke's account of the "First Enrollment". He says that it occurred while Quirinius was administering Syria.

The famous administration of Syria by Quirinius lasted from about AD. 6 to 9; and during that time occurred the" Great Enrollment" and valuation of property in Palestine.[94] Obviously the incidents described by Luke are irreconcilable with that date.

There was found near Tibur (Tivoli) in AD. 1764 a fragment of marble with part of an inscription, which is now preserved in the Lateran Museum of Christian Antiquities, as one of the important monuments bearing on the history of Christianity. The inscription records the career and honors of a Roman official who lived in the reign of Augustus, and survived that emperor. He conquered a nation; he was rewarded with two *Supplicationes* and the *Ornamenta Triumphalia*, *i.e.*, he gorgeous dress of a triumphing general, with ivory scepter and chariot, etc.; he governed Asia as proconsul; and he twice governed Syria as *legatus* of the divine Augustus.

Though the name has perished, yet these indications are sufficient to show with practical certainty (as all the highest authorities are agreed – Mommsen, Borghesi, de Rossi, Henzen, Dessau, and others), that the officer who achieved this splendid career was Publius Sulpicius Quirinius. His government of Syria, AD. 6-9, was therefore his second tenure of that office. He had administered Syria at some previous time. Is not this earlier administration the occasion to which Luke refers?

Here again, however, we are confronted with a serious difficulty. The supreme authority on the subject, Mommsen, considers that the most probable date for Quirinius's first government of Syria is about BC. 3-1; but the question is involved in serious doubts, which Mommsen fully acknowledges. That time is doubly inconsistent with Luke: Herod was dead before it, and it is inconsistent with the whole argument of the preceding pages that the enrollment should have been postponed so long after the periodic year BC. 9.

Again, Luke does not specify exactly what was the Roman office which Quirinius held at the time when this first enrollment was made. The Greek word which he uses ἡγεμονεύοντος τῆς Συρίας Κυρηνίου occurs elsewhere in his History, indicating the office of procurator (Luke 3:1; so ἡγεμών, Acts 23:24, 26, 33; Acts 24:1, 10 and Acts 26:30) and the noun connected with it is even used (Luke 3:1) to indicate the supreme authority exercised by the reigning Emperor in a province.

Hence the word, as employed by Luke, might be applied to any Roman official holding a leading and authoritative position in the province of Syria. It might quite naturally denote some special mission of a high and authoritative nature; and many excellent authorities have argued that Quirinius was dispatched to Syria on some such mission, and that Luke, in assigning the date, mentions him in preference to the regular governor.

We find, then, that uncertainty reigns both as to the date of Quirinius's first governorship, and as to whether Luke called him governor or intended to indicate that he held a special mission in Syria.

Let us now scrutinize closely the evidence bearing on the career of Quirinius. We shall find that, as in so many other cases, a firm grasp of the clue that Luke offers us will guide us safely through a peculiarly entangled problem, and will illuminate a most obscure page of history. The difficulties of the case are due to the contempt in which Luke's testimony has been held by the historians and one school of theologians, and the timorous and faltering belief of others.

The only certain dates in the life of Quirinius are his consulship in BC. 12, his second government of Syria beginning in AD. 6, his prosecution of his former wife, Domitia Lepida, in AD. 20, and his death and public funeral in AD. 21. It is certain that during the eighteen years' interval between his consulship, BC. 12, and his second Syrian administration, AD. 6, the following important events in his career occurred.

PART II. Solution of the Problem

1. He held office in Syria, and carried on war with the Homonadenses, a tribe in the inner mountainous district lying between Phrygia, Cilicia and Lycaonia: he gained in this war successes which were judged so important that two solemn acts of thanksgiving to the gods (*supplicationes*) in Rome were decreed, and the decorations of a triumphing general were awarded to him. The two *supplicationes* were probably awarded for victories in two successive years, for a *supplicatio* was the compliment awarded for a successful campaign, and it is hardly probable that two such compliments would be paid to a general in one year for a single war against one tribe. Moreover, taking into consideration the difficult character of the country where the war occurred, the distance from Syria, the strength of the tribe which had successfully defied the armies of King Amyntas, and the stubborn resistance likely to be offered at point after point and town after town in their large territory, it is quite natural that two campaigns might be required for the whole operations. It is, however, not wholly impossible that two specially brilliant victories may have been gained in one year over the tribe, and that each was thought worthy of a *supplicatio*.

2. Quirinius governed Asia after his first administration of Syria. This was usually an annual office, and the probability therefore is that in his case also it lasted only one year. The exact date is uncertain. We know with great probability that

Asinius Gallus governed Asia in BC. 6-5.

Cn. Lentulus Augur governed Asia in BC. 2-1, also BC. 1-AD. 1 [95]

M. Plautius Silvanus governed Asia in AD. 1-2.

Marcius Censorinus governed Asia in AD. 2-3.

Further, Quirinius was probably in Armenia in AD. 3, as tutor of Gaius Caesar. There are therefore open for Quirinius's tenure of the proconsulship of Asia only the years BC. 5-4, or 4-3, or 3-2, or AD. 4-5, or 5-6.

Again, as M. Waddington, the supreme authority on the subject, points out, the normal interval between the consulship and the proconsulate of Asia during Augustus's reign was five or six years. The only long interval known in that period is twelve years, *viz.*, in the case of Cn.

Lentulus Augur, who was consul BC. 14 and proconsul of Asia BC. 2. It is therefore not probable that Quirinius's proconsulate was postponed over such a long interval as sixteen years (BC. 12 to AD. 4). We therefore conclude that he was probably governor of Asia some years between BC. 5 and 2, and at latest BC. 3-2. Now, his Syrian administration was earlier, and therefore BC. 4-3 is the latest that he can have spent in Syria.

Thus already we find ourselves led to a different opinion from Mommsen's theory.

3. When Lollius, the tutor of Augustus's young grandson Gaius Caesar, who was charged with the arrangement of the Armenian difficulties, died in AD. 2, Quirinius was selected as his successor, obviously on the ground of his great experience in Eastern service. Thereafter he must have spent AD. 3 in Armenia, and probably remained in company with Gaius until the latter, coming back towards Italy wounded and ill, died on the Lycian coast on 21st February, AD. 4.

Zumpt, however, argued that Quirinius was sent to Armenia with Gaius Caesar in BC. 1; and that afterwards Lollius took his place. We follow Mommsen; but it is obvious how difficult and slippery the whole career of Quirinius is, and how slow we should be to condemn Luke for an error in regard to him.

4. Quirinius married Domitia Lepida at some unknown date. He afterwards divorced her, and accused her of attempting to poison him in A. D. 20. Suetonius mentions, as a fact which roused general sympathy for Domitia, that the accusation was brought in the twentieth year after. We ask, "After what?" Common-sense shows Mommsen and others to be right in understanding "the twentieth year after the marriage"; we therefore reject the other interpretation "the twentieth year after the divorce".[96] Mommsen supposes that the marriage was contracted in AD. 4, when Quirinius returned from his honorable duties in Armenia, and that Suetonius makes a great exaggeration when he speaks of the twentieth year. But in such an obscure subject it is surely best to follow the few authorities whom we have, unless they are proved to be inconsistent with known facts. Suetonius is a good authority. Can we not justify him to some extent?

PART II. Solution of the Problem

Domitia Lepida had been betrothed to Augustus's elder grandson, Lucius Caesar, and on his premature death was married to Quirinius. Now Lucius died on 20th August, AD. 2. But the Romans of that period showed the minimum of delicacy in respect of marriages. As soon as the betrothed husband of a wealthy and noble heiress died, the place was open to reward some of Augustus's trusted servants; and no long delay is likely to have occurred in giving her a substitute for Lucius. It is probable that she was married to Quirinius in the autumn of AD. 2, and thus the accusation was brought against her in the nineteenth year (according to Roman methods of counting) from her marriage. In round numbers the populace would talk of "the twentieth year," and thus Suetonius's expression is justified; he professes to be reporting the common talk about the trial.

We conclude, then, that Quirinius was in Rome in the autumn of AD. 2; and was then honored with this grand marriage and the post of guardian to the future emperor, Gaius Caesar. But such honors as this imply that his career in preceding years had been very distinguished. Thus we become still more firmly convinced that his pro-consulate in Asia was past as well as his government of Syria, and that these positions, with the experience in Oriental affairs acquired in them, marked out Quirinius as the proper person to guide the inexperienced Gaius Caesar, and to set right the muddle which had been produced by the headstrong and ill-regulated conduct of Lollius, the previous guardian of the young prince.

These lines of reasoning make it most probable that the two years during which Quirinius was administering Syria and conquering the Homonadenses cannot have been later than BC. 5-3, and may have been earlier.

The same result follows from the consideration that the punishment of the Homonadenses is not likely to have been postponed so late as the years BC. 3-2. The presence of a tribe of barbarians, hostile and victorious, on the frontier of the Roman provinces Galatia and Pamphylia, and adjoining the dependent kingdom of Cilicia Tracheia governed by Archelaos, must have been a source of constant danger. We know that about BC. 6 the pacification of the mountainous Pisidian districts in the south of the Galatic province was proceeding, and the system of military roads was being constructed;[97] and this operation was probably coincident with or even subsequent to the war against the Homonadenses.

But here we find ourselves face to face with the difficulty which has determined Professor Mommsen to place the first Syrian government of Quirinius in BC. 3-1. Quinctilius Varus governed Syria for at least three years, 7-4 BC.: this is rendered quite certain by dated coins of Syrian Antioch struck in his name,[98] and by the statement of Tacitus that he was governing Syria during the disturbances that followed on the death of Herod.[99] Sentius Saturninus certainly governed Syria 9-7 BC., and Josephus says that he was succeeded by Quinctilius Varus.[100] There seems therefore no room for Quirinius›s administration of Syria until we come down as late as BC. 3; yet we have already seen that other lines of argument prompt us to place his Syrian government earlier than that year.

In this difficulty I see no outlet in any direction, whether favorable or unfavorable to Luke, except in the supposition that the foreign relations of Syria, with the command of its armies, were entrusted for a time to Quirinius, with a view to his conducting the difficult and responsible war against the Homonadenses, while the internal administration of the province was left to Saturninus or to Varus (according to the period when we place the mission of Quirinius). This extraordinary command of Quirinius lasted for at least two years, and had come to an end before the death of Herod in BC. 4, for we know on the authority of Tacitus that the disturbances arising in Palestine on that event were put down by Varus; and this trouble, as belonging to the foreign relations of the Province, would on our hypothesis have been dealt with by Quirinius, if he had been still in office.

The question will be put, and must be answered, whether such a temporary division of duties in the Province is in accordance with the Roman Imperial practice. Such a theory is not permissible, unless it is defended by analogous cases and by natural probability. The theory was first suggested to my mind by the analogous case of the African administration, which from the time of Caligula onwards was divided in such a way, that the military power, and with it the foreign policy of the Province, was controlled by a Lieutenant of Augustus,[101] while the internal affairs of the Province were left to the ordinary governor, a Proconsul.

PART II. Solution of the Problem

Almost simultaneously with my papers on the subject there appeared a memoir by Monsieur R. S. Bour,[102] in which he quotes some other analogies to justify this view. He points out that Vespasian conducted the war in Palestine, while Mucianus was governor of Syria, from which Palestine was dependent. Tacitus[103] styles Vespasian *dux*, which is not a strictly official title, but exactly describes his actual duty. He was a Lieutenant of the reigning Emperor Nero,[104] holding precisely the same title and technical rank as Mucianus. We suppose that Quirinius stood in exactly the same relation to Varus as Vespasian in regard to Mucianus. Quirinius was a special Lieutenant of Augustus, who conducted the war against the Homonadenses, while Varus administered the ordinary affairs of Syria. The duties of Quirinius might be described by calling him *dux* in Latin, and the Greek equivalent is necessarily and correctly ἡγεμών, as Luke has it.

Again, Corbulo commanded the armies of Syria in the war against Parthia and Armenia, while Ummidius Quadratus[105] and Cestius Gallus were governors of Syria. Josephus speaks of Gallus, but never mentions the name of Corbulo. We suppose that Quirinius stood in the same relative position as Corbulo, and Josephus preserves the same silence about both.

The chief difference between the view which M. Bour holds and the theory which we advocate is that he distinguishes this position which Quirinius held in BC. 7-6 from the first governorship of Syria, which, like Mommsen, he places after BC. 4. This makes the unnecessary complication that Quirinius first commanded the Syrian armies, then after two or three years governed Syria, and then once more governed Syria. But M. Bour does not observe that even on the first occasion Quirinius was *legatus Augusti*; and it appears quite correct to say that in AD. 6-9 he as *legatus Divi Alugusti iterum Syria obtinuit*, even if he had not been again governor of Syria after BC. 7-6.

Moreover, in the inscription recording the career of (probably) Quirinius, there is no possible space to insert a distinct government of Syria between his successes against the Homonadenses and his second governorship. The inscription clearly implies that the Homonadenses were conquered in his first Syrian administration.

It is a matter of secondary importance that M. Bour supposes Saturninus to have ruled Syria while the enrollment of Palestine was going on, and yet acknowledges that this occurred in BC. 7 or 6. As we have seen, Varus came to govern Syria in the summer of BC. 7. [106]

The conclusion of the whole argument is this.

About BC. 8-5, Augustus made a great effort to pacify the dangerous and troublesome mountaineers of Taurus, to prevent the continual plundering Which they practiced on the peaceable provinces to which they were neighbors, Asia, Galatia and Syria-Cilicia, and to avenge the death of the Roman tributary King of Galatia, Amyntas, in BC. 25. On the one hand the governor of Galatia, on the other hand the governor of Syria, were both required in this work. Part of the mountaineers' country was nominally part of the Province Galatia, having been formerly in the kingdom of Amyntas (which had been transformed into the Province Galatia). But Galatia did not contain an army; and the administration of Syria-Cilicia had always to intervene, when Roman troops were needed during that period on the eastern Roman frontiers.

In BC. 6 the first great step and foundation of the Roman organization was in process of being carried out among the western and northern mountaineers by Cornutus Aquila, governor of Galatia. A military road system was built among them, and a series of garrison-cities (*Coloniae*) was founded, Olbasa, Comama, Cremna, Parlais and Lystra. These fortresses were connected by the Imperial roads[107] with the governing center of Southern Galatia, the great Colonia Caesarea Antiocheia in Southern Phrygia adjoining Pisidia.

About the same time the military operations from the side of Syria were carried out. Josephus tells so much about Saturninus, as to make it clear that he was not engaged in an arduous and difficult war far away in the Taurus mountains, south from Iconium and Lystra. Either the war was later than his time, or it was conducted by a distinct official. As to the official's name there is no doubt. Strabo[108] tells us that it was Quirinius who conquered the Homonadenses and revenged the death of Amyntas. The period is, on the whole, likely to coincide with the connected operations of Cornutus Aquila on the north-western side.

PART II. Solution of the Problem

Accordingly, the probability is that in BC. 7, when Varus came to govern Syria, Augustus perceived that the internal affairs of the province would require all the energy of the regular governor, and sent at the same time a special officer with the usual title, Lieutenant of Augustus, to administer the military resources of the province, and specially to conduct the war against the Homonadenses and any other foreign relations that demanded military intervention. Moreover, Varus had no experience in war; and an experienced officer was needed. Thus, Quirinius conducted the war pretty certainly in BC. 6, perhaps in 7 and 6, perhaps in 6 and 5.

The first periodic enrollment of Syria was made under Saturninus in BC. 8-7. The enrollment of Palestine was delayed by the causes described until the late summer or autumn of BC. 6. At that time, Varus was controlling the internal affairs of Syria, while Quirinius was commanding its armies and directing its foreign policy.

Tertullian, finding that the first periodic enrollment in Syria was made under Saturninus, inferred too hastily that the enrollment in Palestine was made under that governor. With full consciousness and intention, he corrects Luke's statement, and declares that Christ was born during the census taken by Sentius Saturninus. Luke, more accurately, says that the enrollment of Palestine was made while Quirinius was acting as leader (ἡγεμών) in Syria.

The question will perhaps be put whether Luke could rightly describe the authority of Quirinius by the words "holding the *Hegemonia* of Syria». The preceding exposition leaves no doubt on this point. The usage of Luke shows that he regards *Hegemonia* in the provinces as the attribute both of the Emperor and of the officers to whom the Emperor delegates his power. Now that is quite true in point of fact. The Emperor primarily held the supreme authority in Syria (which was one of the Imperatorial provinces, as distinguished from those which were administered by the Senate through the agency of its officers, entitled Proconsuls). But the Emperor could not himself be present in Syria or in Palestine, hence he delegated to substitutes, or Lieutenants, the exercise of his authority in the various provinces which were under his own direct power. These substitutes, when of senatorial rank, bore the title *Legatus Augusti pro prætore*, and when of equestrian rank the title *Procurator cum jure gladii*; but both *Legati* and *Procuratores* are called by Luke *Hegemones*, as exercising the *Hegemonia* that belongs to the Emperor.

Now Quirinius was exercising this delegated *Hegemonia* over the armies of the Province Syria, and it seems quite in keeping with Luke›s brief pregnant style to say that he held the *Hegemonia* of Syria.

But why did Luke not name Varus, the ordinary governor, in place of dating by the extraordinary officer? If he had had regard to the susceptibilities of modern scholars, and the extreme dearth of knowledge about the period, which was to exist 1800 years after he wrote, he would certainly have named Varus. But he was writing for readers who could as easily find out about Quirinius as about Varus, and he had no regard for us of the nineteenth century. Quirinius ruled for a shorter time than Varus, and he controlled the foreign relations of the province, hence he furnished the best means of dating.

But why did Luke not distinguish clearly between this enrollment and the later enrollment of A. D. 7, which was held by Quirinius in Syria and in Palestine? We answer that he does distinguish, accurately and clearly. He tells that this was the first enrollment of the series, but the moderns are determined to misunderstand him. They insist that Luke confused the use of comparative and superlative in Greek, and that we cannot take the full force of the word "first" as "first of many". They go on to put many other stumbling-blocks in the way, but none of these cause any difficulty if we hold fast to the fundamental principle that Luke was a great historian who wrote good Greek of the first century kind.

NOTE 1

Quinctilius Varus, governor of Syria. The exact date is shown by the coins of Antioch, which bear the numbers κε, κϛ´, κζ´ of the Actian era, accompanied by the name of Varus. Now the battle of Actium was fought on 2nd September, 31. When such an event was taken as an era, the years were not (as was formerly assumed by many authorities) made to begin from the anniversary of the event. The years went on as before; but the current year in which the event occurred was reckoned the year

PART II. Solution of the Problem

1. Hence, in countries where the Greek year common in the Aegean lands, beginning at the autumn equinox, was employed, the year 1 of the Actian era was BC. 32-31 (beginning 24th September, 32).

But that system could not be the one which was employed in reckoning the Actian years at Antioch, for the year 26 in that case would end in the autumn of BC. 6. Now, coins of the Actian year 26 mention the twelfth consulship of Augustus, which did not begin till 1st January, BC. 5; similarly coins of the year 29 (ending on that system in autumn BC. 3) mentioned the thirteenth consulship of Augustus, which did not begin until 1st January, BC. 2.

The Actian years in Antioch were therefore reckoned by a system in which the years began before 2nd September. It is probable that the year which was sometimes used in Syria, beginning on 18th April, may have been employed also in Antioch. But whatever the exact day of New Year was, the following table shows the system of Actian years in Antioch: –

Actian year 1 ended in spring (perhaps 17 th April), BC. 30
Actian year 25 ended in spring (perhaps 17 th April), BC. 6
Actian year 27 ended in spring (perhaps 17 th April), BC. 4
Actian year 29 ended in spring (perhaps 17 th April), BC. 2

Varus, therefore, came to Syria at such a time that coins marked 25 were struck after his arrival, *i.e.*, he arrived probably soon after midsummer of that year, *i.e.*, July to September, BC. 7. He remained in Syria until at least the midsummer of BC. 4, some months after the death of Herod.

NOTE 2

The theory has also been advanced that Quirinius was one of a number of commissioners, appointed by Augustus to hold the enrollment throughout the Roman world, Quirinius being the commissioner for Syria and Palestine. In this capacity, also, Quirinius would be a delegate exercising the Emperor's authority, *Legattts Augusti*; and therefore he might rightly be said by Luke ἡγεμονεύειν τῆς Συρίας This theory is possible; it offends against no principle of Roman procedure or of language. It may be the truth. But, on the whole, it seems to have less in its favor than the one which has been advocated in the text. M. R. S. Bour[109] judges of it exactly as I have done. It was advocated in the summer of 1897 by Signor O. Marucchi in the Italian review Bessarione.

---

[94] Acts 5:37; Josephus, *Ant. Jud.*, 17., 13; 18., 1, 1.

[95] Lentulus was in office in Asia on 10th May, BC. 1, and therefore, as Mommsen says, governed during the year 2-1 (*Res Gestae D. Aug.*, p. 170). But, as Waddington sees (*Fastes d'Asie*, p. 101), Lentulus seems to have been still in office on 12th August, and therefore probably ruled Asia also in the year 1 BC. – 1 AD.

[96] Mr. Furneaux takes the latter sense in his admirable edition of Tacitus, *Annals*, 3., 23, and so apparently does Nipperdey also; and it must be acknowledged that Suetonius's expression suits that. Sense and the historical facts, however, show it to be impossible.

[97] See my *Church in the Roman Empire*, p. 32; C. I. L., 3., No. 6974.

[98] See Note 1 at the end of Chapter 11.

[99] Probably about 1st April, BC. 4.

[100] *Ant. Jud.*, 17., 5, 2.

[101] *Legatus Augusti pro praetore.*

[102] See Note 2 at the end of Chapter 11.

[103] Hist., 1., 10.

[104] Legatus Augusti pro praetore.

[105] He was unfit for the war, Mommsen, *Röm. Gesch.*, 5., 382 f. Corbulo governed Syria for a time after Quadratus; but the burden apparently was too great, and Gallus was appointed.

[106] M. Bour also finds an allusion to the universal enrollment in a phrase of the *Monumentum Ancyranum* where the restored text was *omnium prov[inciarum censure egi or statum ordinav*i]; but he has not remarked that the recovered Greek translation proves the sense and words to have been *omnium prov[inciarum Populi Romani]... fines auxi.*

[107] βασιλικαὶ ὁδοί, *Church in Rom. Emp.*, p. 32; Lanckoronski, *Städte Pamphyliens*, 2., p. 203.

[108] Strabo, p. 569. His account certainly suggests both that the revenge was not delayed so late as Mommsen›s view implies, and that a good deal of time was needed to carry out all the operations involved, the foundation of new cities, the transference of population, etc.

[109] *L'Inscription de Quirinius et le Recensement de St. Luc*, Rome, 1897: a treatise crowned by the *Pontificia Accademia di Archeologia*. This skillful argument was presented to the Academy in Dec., 1806, and published in the late summer or autumn of 1897. It refers in a concluding note to my papers on the same subject in *Expositor*, April and June, 1897.

PART III.
SOME ASSOCIATED QUESTIONS

Chapter 12.
SOME ASSOCIATED QUESTIONS

A BRIEF reference to some of the other difficulties, which have been found in Luke's references to matters of contemporary history, will form a fitting conclusion to this study.

In some cases all that is wanted to solve the difficulty is proper understanding of Luke's words. That, for example, is the case with Acts 11:28, where the statement, that in the days of Claudius there was famine over all the world, has been misinterpreted to imply that harvests failed and a famine ensued in every part of the whole world at exactly the same time, which would be an obvious exaggeration, and therefore not entirely trustworthy: it would be quite in the rhetorical style of Tacitus or Juvenal, not in the simple and true manner of Luke.

But, as all the commentators have pointed out, Suetonius, Dion Cassius, Tacitus and Eusebius mention scarcity occurring at different times in widely scattered parts of the Roman world during that reign; and an inscription has been interpreted (though not with certainty) as referring to a famine in Asia Minor some years before AD. 56. [110] At no period in Roman history are so many allusions to widespread famine found as under Claudius. Luke refers to what must then have been an accepted belief, that at some time or other during the reign of Claudius every part of the Roman world suffered from famine.

A much more difficult case occurs in Acts 5:36-37, where Gamaliel in addressing the Sanhedrin says: "Before these days rose up Theudas, giving himself out to be somebody, to whom a number of men, about 400, joined themselves, who was slain, and all, as many as obeyed him, were dispersed and came to naught. And after this man rose up *Judas the Galilean in the days of the enrollment'* and caused people to revolt under his leadership: he also perished; and all, as many as obeyed him, were scattered abroad.»

Now Josephus describes "a certain magician, named Theudas, who, while Fadus was Procurator of Judea, persuaded most of the people τὸν

PART III. Some Associated Questions

πλεῖστον ὄχλον to take up their property and follow him to the river Jordan; for he told them he was a prophet, and he said that he would divide the river by his command and afford them easy passage through it; and he deceived many by telling them this. Fadus, however, did not permit them to profit by their folly, but sent a squadron of cavalry against them, which falling unexpectedly upon them, slew many of them and captured many alive. And they took Theudas himself alive and cut off his head and brought it to Jerusalem "(*Ant Jud.*, 20., 5, 1).

In the following paragraph Josephus describes what happened under the government of Tiberius Alexander, the successor of Fadus; and, among other things, he tells that "the sons of *Judas the Galilean* were slain, *viz.*, that Judas who *caused the people to revolt* from the Romans when *Quirinius was making the valuation* of Judea».

It is pointed out that in two successive paragraphs Josephus speaks first of Theudas and then of Judas, dating the latter under Quirinius; and that in two successive verses Luke speaks first of Theudas and then of Judas, dating the latter at the great enrollment (*i.e.*, under Quirinius). From this the inference is drawn that Luke, reading hurriedly and carelessly the passage of Josephus, falsely inferred that Theudas, who is mentioned first, was the elder; and they point to the analogy, between the two accounts of Judas,[111] as evidence that Luke borrowed from Josephus.

Finally, since Josephus's Theudas rose and fell several years after Gamaliel is supposed to have delivered his speech, they infer that Luke had no authority for the words which he puts into Gamaliel's mouth, but freely invented the whole according to a common practice among ancient historians. Luke, as they say, constructed a suitable speech for Gamaliel out of his own scrappy and inaccurate reading, and thus made Gamaliel describe an event that had not yet occurred, supposing it to have taken place before AD. 6.

Without doubt, if this theory is correct, we must throw up our whole case as hopeless. The blunder attributed to Luke is so ingeniously many-sided as to destroy his credit in various directions. It shows that he invented his speeches without authority; that he was incapable of reading two short paragraphs of Greek without misunderstanding them; that, even when he had a good authority before him, he could not report his information without introducing a portentous blunder; that he was so ignorant of Judean history as to think that an event which Josephus dates under Fadus could be, in the first place, older than Gamaliel's speech (delivered soon after AD. 29 or 30), and, in the second place, older than the great enrollment. The most wretched old chronicler, in the worst and most ignorant Byzantine time, has not succeeded in doing anything so bad as that. To find a parallel instance of ignorance and stupidity, where knowledge is professed and must be expected, one must come down to modern times and look in the papers of rejected candidates in a "pass" examination, who have vainly tried, with the minimum of care and work, to delude the examiner into the belief that they know enough to be permitted to scrape through the test.

But is not this too gross a blunder? Is it credible that a person who was so shockingly ignorant and inaccurate should aspire to be a historian? The aspirations of men are usually Founded on the conscious possession of some qualifications for success. Luke evidently aimed – and probably was the first to aim – at connecting the story of the development of Christianity with the course of general Imperial history. Surely he would not have aimed at doing so, unless he possessed a certain moderate knowledge of that history. In his preface he declares that his motive for writing his work was that he was in possession of such exceptionally excellent information, gained from first-rate authorities. But only the grossest incapacity and ignorance combined could have enabled him to succeed in attaining so colossal a blunder.

The theory seems to me incredible, irrational, and psychologically impossible. It is irreconcilable with the known facts and the character of Luke's History; and I am confident that if it had been stated about any writer who was not a Christian, it would have been universally treated with the contempt that it merits. It is the sort of fancy that brands its originator and its believer as either lacking the critical faculty or blinded by prejudice.

Moreover, the theory is founded on an accidental peculiarity of order in the text of Josephus, and presupposes that Luke was indebted entirely to one passage of Josephus for his knowledge of Theudas and Judas. He could hardly have read any additional authority without acquiring some more correct idea as to the time when Theudas lived.

It is not here the place to discuss the question whether Luke had read Josephus. As Dr. Sanday[112] says, the assumption that he used the Jewish Antiquities «rests on little more than the fact that both writers relate or allude to the same events, though the differences between them are really more marked than the resemblances». He adds that «Schuerer[113] sums up the controversy by saying that either Luke had taken no notice of Josephus at all, which he thinks the simpler and more probable supposition, or at once forgot everything that he had read». The latter opinion is that of a scholar who believes Luke to have written after Josephus. We hold Luke to have written before him.

In truth there is between Luke and Josephus the minimum of resemblance and the maximum of discrepancy possible between two authorities writing about the same period, and both (as we believe) enjoying access to excellent authorities.

Moreover, it is clear, on the recognized principles of critical study, that Luke used some other authority and was not indebted to Josephus alone; for he mentions the exact number of persons who followed Theudas, *viz.*, 400, whereas Josephus would lead one to believe that Theudas had a very much larger following.[114] Thus Luke had other means of learning the date of Theudas. It may be answered that Luke invented the number, and designedly or through incapacity varied from the account that Josephus gives. To that no reply need be given: they who say so will be ready to declare that Luke, who could read Josephus and suppose the procurator Fadus to be older than the great enrollment, was equally capable of reading any number of additional authorities without profiting by them!

We cannot, it is true, tell who was the Theudas to whom Gamaliel refers. The period is very obscure; Josephus is practically our only authority. He does not allude, or profess to allude, to every little disturbance on the banks of the Jordan. There is no real difficulty in believing that more than one impostor may have borne or taken the name Theudas;

that one Theudas, amid the troubles that followed the death of Herod the Great (a period about which we have no information except that there were great troubles, calling for the presence of a Roman army from the Province Syria), or at some earlier time, pretended to be somebody, and found 400 followers; and that another Theudas, about AD. 44-46, called himself a prophet, and led after him a great part of the Jewish people.

The result is, at present, disappointing. We have to leave the difficulty unsolved. We must hope for the discovery of further evidence. Meantime, no one who finds Luke to be a trustworthy historian in the rest of his History will see any difficulty in this passage.

But there is good cause to look forward confidently to the progress of discovery. The advance in knowledge, due to the increased activity in searching, has been immense during recent years. The whole essay, which has been here set before the public, is founded on one discovery; and after it was print it has been confirmed by a new find.[115]

We may suitably conclude the essay with another discovery, slight in itself, but significant of the general trend of advancing knowledge.[116]

The reference in Acts 10:1 to an Italic Cohort (of which Cornelius was a centurion) has caused some difficulty and discussion in recent years. Some excellent scholars have entertained the suspicion that this detail is an anachronism, caused by the intrusion of circumstances that were true at a later time into this early period. It is established by an inscription that an Italic Cohort was stationed in Syria at a considerably later time; and the theory is that Luke, knowing that such a Cohort was there at the time when he wrote, either incorrectly added this detail to the story which he learned about Cornelius, or in some other way manipulated or invented the story. What reason he had for so treating the story, and how precisely he treated it, the theory does not state. It simply casts discredit in a vague way on the story, accusing it of containing a false detail.[117]

Among non-theologians, Professor Mommsen pronounces no judgment, but avoids making any positive suggestion about the Cohort, in his illuminative paper in the Sitzungsberichte of the Berlin Academy, 1895, p. 503.[118] Marquardt, in the work from which all study must always begin in these subjects, Romische Staatsverwaltung, 2., p. 467, note 5, accepts the words of Acts as an ordinary authority, quoting them along with other references to an Italic Cohort. A recent discovery confirms the position taken by Marquardt, and will probably be held by most scholars as a sufficient proof that, in our present state of knowledge, the suspicion that has been entertained about the reference is contrary to the balance of evidence.

Dr. Bormann[119] publishes an inscription found recently at Carnuntum, one of the great military stations in Pannonia, on the south bank of the Danube, a little below Vienna. It is the epitaph of a young soldier, Proculus, a subordinate officer (*optio*) in the second Italic Cohort, who died at Carnuntum while engaged on detached service from the Syrian army (as an officer in a corps of archers from Syria, temporarily sent on special service and encamped at Carnuntum).[120] Proculus was born at Philadelphia (doubtless the city of that name beyond Jordan, the old Rabbath-Ammon), and his father bore the Syrian name Rabilus.

As to the date of this epitaph, Bormann and Domaszewski, two of the highest authorities, have come independently to the same conclusion. The epitaph was found with a group of others, stamped by criteria derived both from nomenclature, and from inscriptional and alphabetical character, as belonging to the period of the early emperors. This group belongs to all older cemetery, which was in use before AD. 73, when a new camp near Carnuntum was built for the soldiers stationed there. Further, the service on which these Syrian soldiers had come to Carnuntum can be dated with the highest probability.

In AD. 69, Syrian detachments to the number of 13,000 men swelled the army which Mucianus, governor of Syria, led westwards to support Vespasian in his struggle against Vitellius. But before Mucianus arrived on the scene, the armies of Pannonia and Moesia had declared for Vespasian, marched into Italy, and finished the contest. Their departure had left the northern frontier undefended against the barbarians, Dacians, Germans, etc., beyond the Danube. As Tacitus mentions, the Dacians showed signs of invading Moesia, and Mucianus dispatched the Sixth Legion[121] to guard against them on the Lower Danube. Tacitus does not say anything about the Upper Danube; but there also the danger was so obvious, that an experienced governor like Mucianus could hardly fail to send a guard thither also; for the words of Tacitus (*Hist.*, 3., 46) show that he was fully alive to the danger all along the northern frontier. In this way we may conclude that part of the detachments came to Carnuntum; and there Proculus died, perhaps in AD. 70. The Syrian armies were evidently soon sent back to the East, where the Sixth Legion is shortly afterwards mentioned as engaged in operations in the northern parts of Syria in 73.

There was therefore an Italic Cohort stationed in Syria in AD. 69. It was recruited from Syria,[122] and therefore, according to the principle laid down by Mommsen, it belonged to the eastern Roman armies. It is therefore in every way probable that an Italic Cohort was stationed in the Province Syria, as Dr. Bormann has observed, about AD. 40, when Cornelius is mentioned as «a centurion of the Cohort called Italic,» resident in Caesarea (the Roman governmental center of Palestine).

This discovery, it is true, does not prove conclusively that the Italic Cohort, which had been stationed in Syria before AD. 69, was there as early as about AD. 40. It is not beyond the range of possibility that the Cohort might have been sent to Syria between 40 and 69. Movements of troops from province to province were not rare, and the Italic Cohort might have been moved in that interval. But, in general, the movements were caused by military requirements which can be ascertained. As Marquardt says of Syria, "the same Legions remained for centuries in the province," and they were divided between many different stations, not massed in single centers: for example, detachments of the Third Legion called Gallica, can be traced in Sidon, Beirut, Aera in the district Auranitis, and Phaena in Trachonitis. The whole burden of proof, therefore, rests with those who maintain that a Cohort which was in Syria before 69 was not there in 40. There is a strong probability that Luke is right when he alludes to that Cohort as part of the Syrian garrison about AD. 40.

A series of arguments have been advanced to buttress this assumption that Luke when he spoke of an Italic Cohort in Syria about 40 was guilty of an anachronism.

It is pointed out, in the first place, that between AD. 41 and 44, during which period Judea was formed into a dependent kingdom ruled

PART III. Some Associated Questions

by Herod Agrippa, a Roman Cohort would not be stationed in Caesarea. If this were certain, it would merely confirm the view taken by many scholars that the incident of Cornelius occurred earlier than 41. But as a matter of fact we know far too little of the relations between the rule of Agrippa and the provincial administration to be sure that a centurion would not be resident in Caesarea during his short reign. There is nothing more obscure than the precise terms on which the numerous dependent kingdoms in Asia Minor and Syria were administered. It is practically certain that these subject kingdoms were tributary from the first, even when they had never before been subject to Rome; and even Herod the Great's action was controlled by Rome in many important respects, and his subjects took an oath to be faithful to the Romans. But the Judean kingdom of Agrippa, as it existed in AD. 41-44, had long been actually part of a Roman province; and there is great probability that it might retain certain relations with the provincial government, and that officers of the provincial soldiery might be kept resident in the capital, Caesarea, to maintain these relations. There is much that might be said on this point; but it is not necessary for our main purpose. Moreover, the whole subject is so obscure that a scholar who aims simply at understanding the subject will at present refrain from any dogmatic statement about it, and will certainly be very slow to condemn an ancient author for inaccuracy, because he does not confirm the modern scholar's hasty conjecture. All that need be said is that at present we find the argument so devoid of force that it hardly even affords any presumption in favor of a date for the incident of Cornelius earlier than AD. 41.

In the next place it has been argued that even between AD. 6 and 41, when Judea was part of the Province Syria, and when Roman auxiliary troops were stationed both at Caesarea and at Jerusalem, an Italic Cohort cannot have been stationed at Caesarea. This assertion is based on a series of conjectures as to the Roman forces stationed in Judea during these years. It is fortunately unnecessary for me to discuss these conjectures: I need only point out

(1) that they are in direct contradiction to the principles previously laid down by Mommsen, the supreme authority on the subject;[123]

(2) that Mommsen has now considered them and judged them to be "erroneous in every respect".[124]

But, further, even supposing that these conjectures were strong enough to support the conclusion that the Italic Cohort was not stationed in Caesarea, we know far too little to justify the inference that a centurion of that Cohort could not be on duty there, detached from his Cohort on special service. The entire subject of detachment-service is most obscure; and. we are very far from being able to say with certainty that the presence of an auxiliary centurion[125] in Caesarea is impossible, unless the Cohort in which he was an officer was stationed there.

Since the question of the Roman troops in Palestine is so full of difficulties, that it is hardly possible to make any assertion in the matter, what judgment should be pronounced on the light-heartedness which suspects Luke of inaccuracy, because he does not conform to the conjectures which some distinguished German professor sets forth? It is a matter of interest to observe how slow some very learned New Testament scholars are to appreciate the principle, which is regarded as fundamental by the historical and antiquarian students, that no conjecture which is not founded on clear evidence has any right even to be propounded, if it contradicts the direct statement of an ancient authority. Much less ought the ancient authority to be discredited because he disagrees with a loose and disputed modern conjecture.

The episode of Cornelius in Acts is characterized by that vagueness and want of direct, incisive statement of details, which Luke shows in handling the early history of the Church in Palestine. He was not at home in the province of Syria, and the Jewish people in particular he neither understood nor liked. If the narrative of Cornelius showed the same mastery of facts and surroundings as is apparent in Philippi or Ephesus or Cyprus or Athens, we should find it far more instructive than it is as to the way in which an officer of the Roman army of occupation lived. Was he resident in a private house? How was he in such close relations with the Jews throughout Palestine? Many questions suggest themselves, pressing for an answer, which I cannot give. But the tendency of discovery distinctly is, in this as in other cases, to confirm the trustworthiness of the general situation.

---

[110] *St. Paul the Traveller*, p. 48 f.

[111] ἐν ταῖς ἡμέραις τῆς ἀπογραφῆς καὶ ἀπέστησε λαὸν ὀπί σω αὐτοῦ in Luke, and τὸν λαὸν ἀπὸ ἀποστήσαντος Κυρινίου τῆς Ἰουδαίς τιμητεύοντος in Josephus.

[112] *Bampton Lectures*, 1893, p. 278.

[113] *Lucas und Josephus* in *Zeitschr. f. krit. Theologie*, 1876, p. 574 ff. Josephus's great work on the *Jewish Antiquities* was written about AD. 93-94.

[114] πείθει τὸν πλεῖστον ὄχλον . . . ἔπεσθα are his words.

[115] See Preface.

[116] The following paragraphs are shortened and modified (but without altering the opinions stated) from an article in the *Expositor*, September, 1896.

[117] *Steht . . . unter dem Verdacht, Verhaltnisse einer spaterer Zeit in eine fruhere zuruck verlegt zu haben.*

[118] *Mit Sicherheit vermoegen wir weder diese* cohors Augusta (Acts 27:1) *noch die* σπεῖρα Ἰταλική *. . . zu identificieren.*

[119] *Archaol. Epigr. Mittheil. aus Oesterreich*, 1895, p. 218.

[120] *Ex vexil. sagit. exer. Syriaci*, where Bormann's completion of the abbreviations seems beyond question *ex vexillariis sagittariis exercitus Syriaci*.

[121] This Legion, called. Ferrata, was enrolled by Augustus and stationed in Syria. It formed part of Mucianus's army in AD. 69; and it remained in Judea at least as late as the third century.

[122] Proculus was in his seventh year of service when he died, and had probably enlisted in AD. 64 (when he was nineteen years old).

[123] See Mommsen in *Hermes*, 19., p. 217.

[124] *In jeder Hinsicht verfehlt*, Mommsen in *Berlin. Akad. Sitz.* 1895, p. 501.

[125] Auxiliary centurions, being of lower rank than legionary, were not employed as *frumentarii* (like Julius in Acts 27.); but there were other ways of detached service.

Appendix 1.

THE INSCRIPTION OF QUIRINIUS
(LAPIS TIBURTINUS)

GEM · QVA · REDACTA · INPOI AVGVSTI · POPVLIQVE
· ROMANI · SENATV SVPPLICATIONES · BINAS · OB
SVPPLICATIONES · RES · PROSP IPSI · ORNAMENTA ·
TRIVMPI PRO · CONSVL SVPPLICATIONES · ASIAM ·
PROVINCIAM · OP DIVI · AVGVSTI SVPPLICATIONES ·
ITERVM · SYRIAM · ET · PH

The following restoration is often doubtful: –
*P. Sulpicius P. F. Quirinius cos., datus rector Gaio
Caesari Divi Augusti nepot* . . . .

. . . .

*Pr., pro consule Cretam et Cyrenas provinciam
optinens Marmaridas et Garamantas subegit*

. . . .

*Legatus pro praetore Divi Augusti Syriacas legiones
optinens bellum gessit cum gente Homonadensium
quae interfecerat Amyntam Galatarum*
regem, qua redacta in *potestatem Imp. Caesaris*
Augusti Populique Romani, Senatus *dis immortalibus*
supplicationes binas ob res prosp*ere ab eo gestas, et*
ipsi ornamenta triumph *alia decrevit*
Proconsul Asiam provinciam *optinuit, legatus pr. pr.*
Divi Augusti iterum Syriam et *Phoenicen provinciam
optinens regnum Archelai in provinciae formam redegit.*

Appendix 1.

THE INSCRIPTION OF QUIRINIUS
(LAPIS TIBURTINUS)

GEM · QVA · REDACTA · INPOI AVGVSTI · POPVLIQVE
· ROMANI · SENATV SVPPLICATIONES · BINAS · OB
SVPPLICATIONES · RES · PROSP IPSI · ORNAMENTA ·
TRIVMPI PRO · CONSVL SVPPLICATIONES · ASIAM ·
PROVINCIAM · OP DIVI · AVGVSTI SVPPLICATIONES ·
ITERVM · SYRIAM · ET · PH

The following restoration is often doubtful: –
*P. Sulpicius P. F. Quirinius cos., datus rector Gaio
Caesari Divi Augusti nepot* . . . .
 .   .   .   .   .

*Pr., pro consule Cretam et Cyrenas provinciam
optinens Marmaridas et Garamantas subegit*
 .   .   .   .

*Legatus pro praetore Divi Augusti Syriacas legiones
optinens bellum gessit cum gente Homonadensium
quae interfecerat Amyntam Galatarum*
regem, qua redacta in *potestatem Imp. Caesaris*
Augusti Populique Romani, Senatus *dis immortalibus*
supplicationes binas ob res prosp*ere ab eo gestas, et*
ipsi ornamenta triumph *alia decrevit*
Proconsul Asiam provinciam *optinuit, legatus pr. pr.*
Divi Augusti iterum Syriam et *Phoenicen provinciam
optinens regnum Archelai in provinciae formam redegit.*

Appendix 2.

THE INSCRIPTION OF AEMILIUS SECUNDUS
(LAPIS VENETUS)

Q · AEMILIVS · · Q · F
PAL · SECVNDVS *in*
CASTRIS · DIVI · AVG · · *Sub*
P · SVLPIcIO · QVIRINIO · LE*gaug*.
5 CaESARIS · SYRIAE · HONORI
BVS · DECORATVS · PRaEFECT
COHORT · AVG · I · PRaEFECT
COHORT · II · CLASSICAE · IDEM
IVSSV · QVIRINI · CENSVM · EGI
10 APAMENAE · CIVITATIS · MIL
LIVM · HOMIN · CIVIVM · CXVII
IDEM · MISSV · QVIRINI · ADVERSVS
ITVRAEOS · IN · LIBANO · MONTE ·
CASTELLVM · EORVM · CEPI · ET · ANTE
15 MILITIEM · PRAEFECT · FABRVM ·
DELATVS · A · DVOBVS · COS · AD · AE
RARIVMET · IN · COLONIA ·
QVAESTOR · AEDIL · II · DVVMVIR · II
PONTIFEXS
20 IBI · POSITI · SVNT · Q · AEMILIVS · Q · F · PAL
SECVNDVS · F · ET · AEMILIA · CHIA · LIB
H · M · AMPLIVS · H · N · S

Appendix 3.

THE ITALIC COHORT INSCRIPTION
(LAPIS CARNUNTENSIS)

PROCVLVS
RABILI·F·COL
PHILADEL·MIL·
OPTIO·COH·II
ITALIC·C·R·F
TINI·EX·VEXIL·SA
GIT·EXER·SYRIACI
STIP·VII·VIXIT·AN
    XXVI
APVLEIVS·FRATE
  F·   C·

Proculus Rabili f (ilius)
Col(lina) Philadel(phia)
mil(es) optio coh(ortis) II
Italic(ae) c(ivium) R(omanorurn
centuria) F[aus] tini,
ex vexil(lariis?) sagit(tariis?)
exer(citus) Syriaci
stip(endiorum) VII; vixit
an(nos) XXVI. Apuleius
frate(r) f(aciundum) c(uravit).

Appendix 4.

RATING PAPER: Ἀπογραφή

Μητροδώρωι ἐπιμελητῆι
παρὰ Ἀπύγχιος Ἰναρώτιος
ἑλληνομεμφίτης ^sic^ Ἀπογράφομαι
κατὰ τὸ ἐκτεθὲν πρόσταγμα
τὴν ὑπάρχυσάν ^sic^ μοι οἰκίαν
καὶ αὐλὴ ^sic^ ἐν τῶν Ἑλληνίωι ἐν τόπωι Ἰμενσθὼτ
ἱερῶι, ἧς μέτρα τῆς μὲν οἰκίας π(ήχεις) κα ἐπὶ π(ήχεις) ιγ
τῆς δὲ αὐλῆς π(ήχεις) δ ἐπὶ π(ήχεις) [. . .],
γείτονες πρὸς νότον οἰκία Ταυψάιτος
Φανῶτος, πρὸς βορρᾶν Πάσιτος ἀριάνιος
καὶ ὁδὸς ἀνὰ μέσον, πρὸς λίβα
σιτοποεῖόν μου καὶ ὁδὸς ἀνὰ μέσον,
πρὸς ἀπηλιώτην Ποκαὺς Πετεπτ. ν. ος.
Ταύτην οὖν τιμῶμαι (παχμῶν) δ΄ (=400).
Καὶ ἄλλην οἰκίαν, ἐν ᾗ σιτοποιοῦσιν
καὶ αὐλὴ, ^sic^ ὧν μέτρα τῆς μὲν οἰκίας
μέτρα π(ήχεις) κα ἐπὶ π(ήχεις) ιγ, καὶ τῆς αὐλῆς π(ήχεις) δ
ἐπι π(ήχεις) ιγ, γείτονες Ὀννῶφρις Ὥρου οἰκίας,
πρὸς βορρᾶν Πάσιτος τοῦ Ἀριάνοις καὶ ὁδὸς
ἀνὰ μέσον, πρὸς λίβα Νεφεργήριος
Παχράτου, πρὸς ἀπηλιώτην ἡ προγεγραμένη ^sic^
οἰκία καὶ ὁδὸς ἀνὰ μέσον. Ταύην οὖν
τιμῶμαι χαλκοῦ (δραχμῶν) β΄ (=2000)
  / τά(λαντον) α.

www.ingramcontent.com/pod-product-compliance
Lightning Source LLC
LaVergne TN
LVHW051603070426
835507LV00021B/2742